GW00788075

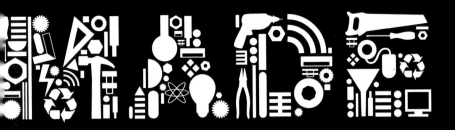

By Steve Rowland
& Bianca Donnelly

First published in 2008 by *Made in ...*

Copyright © Steve Rowland
and Bianca Donnelly 2008
Book Design © Steve Rowland 2008

ISBN 9780955859410

9 780955 859410

Medway

COUNCIL

Serving You

Medway is the largest conurbation in the south-east, situated in the heart of the North Kent Thames Gateway. It has a population of over 250,000, with an economy worth more than £2.8 billion per year.

The number of businesses in Medway has increased by 25 per cent since 2000 and there are now more than 13,000. Over 800 businesses operate in manufacturing and engineering, a major sector focus for Medway's economic development plans. It also has a sharp focus on innovation and support for innovative businesses. Combined with its extensive higher-education sector, Medway has the ingredients to make it a leading high-quality manufacturing and engineering hub for the south-east and the UK.

BAE SYSTEMS

BAE Systems is the premier global defence and aerospace company delivering a full range of products and services for air, land and naval forces as well as advanced electronics, information-technology solutions and customer-support services. With approximately 100,000 employees worldwide, BAE Systems' sales exceeded £15.7 billion (US $31.4 billion) in 2007.

Platform Solutions is a transatlantic business, part of the Electronics, Intelligence and Support operating group, that serves the defence and aerospace communities with capabilities and products that improve operational safety and enhance mission effectiveness.

The business supports a wide range of military and commercial platforms – including fixed and rotary-wing aircraft and ground vehicles – with capabilities in vehicle management, human–machine interface and power management.

south east

mas

BERR manufacturing advisory service

The Manufacturing Advisory Service (MAS) South East is a publicly funded organisation dedicated to providing straightforward practical advice and hands-on support to improve performance and add value to the bottom line of manufacturers in the region. MAS South East aims to improve the efficiency and effectiveness of manufacturers to create sustainable improvements. Through our team of experienced practitioners, each with a strong manufacturing background, we provide tailored support to suit the individual requirements of a business as we guide you through the processes of business improvement to produce real results.

MAS South East - encouraging manufacturing competitiveness in today's global market.

▪M▪E▪P▪

Medway Economic Partnership

The Medway Economic Partnership's (MEP) collective voice strives to ensure Medway is competitive and maintains a vibrant economy. It is a strategic consultation group represented by Medway Council, Medway's major employers, business representatives and key stakeholders within Medway. The MEP is also one of the five lead bodies of Medway's Local Strategic Partnership.

The MEP's representatives provide economic direction for Medway, providing their views on matters of local, regional and national importance – they are also consulted to inform, monitor and comment on the Medway Economic Development Strategy, the Learning and Skills Plan, the Regional Economic Strategy and other key documents that help to shape Medway's future.

UCA Rochester is part of a network of creative industries that contribute to Rochester's growing reputation as a city of culture, learning and new technologies. Our students can choose from a wide range of disciplines, including art and design, photography and fashion. Studying at UCA within an exciting community of artists and designers equips our students with skills, opportunities and possibilities for creative, personal and professional development. As well as leading academic excellence we are keen to provide support for those looking to set up or progress into working within the creative industries.

The School of Engineering, based at the Medway Campus of the University of Greenwich, offers the business community a wide range of services to support and enhance manufacturing operations and productivity. This ranges from high level expertise and facilities such as rapid prototyping, reverse engineering and leading-edge machine-tool capability available through the Renishaw Centre for Manufacturing Productivity. This is complemented by advanced computer-aided engineering and product lifecycle software tools for design, manufacturing and quality management through the Centre for Innovative Product Development. These initiatives are supported by short-course provision for business and a range of first degree and Masters level programmes.

Tonic: Creative Business Project mixes creativity and business in a range of free, innovative courses. The project aims to inject creativity into business and to offer business skills to creatives. Tonic is funded by the Kent and Medway Lifelong Learning Network and is a collaborative project between the University for the Creative Arts at Rochester, the University of Kent, Canterbury Christ Church University and has the support of other colleges across the county. All courses are accredited, taken from higher education programmes and offered at times to suit those in work to support lifelong learning through access to higher education.

Written by
Bianca Donnelly
Zoe Hatton
Art Direction and Design
Steve Rowland
Photography
Rikard Österlund
Chris Marchant
Contributors
Simon Pruciak
Simon Smith
Mike Rutherford
Lauren Hulbert

We would like to thank the following
for their contribution:
Wayne Saunders from Economic
Development, Medway Council,
Dianne Taylor-Gearing from UCA
and Declan Rowland.

Everyone who has supported the book,
got involved and all the featured
companies for believing it wasn't
another 'sales call'.

Slide
to
open

Medway

'A good motorway network and excellent access to the Continent by road/rail.'

'Excellent transport infrastructure.'

'Communications are good with the motorway and airports.'

'Close proximity and communication links to mainland Europe.'

'Excellent location for road networks.'

'Location is excellent, it has convenient access to London and the Continent.'

'The commercial world thought him extravagant; but although he was so, great things are not done by those who sit down and count the cost of every thought and act.' Daniel Gooch on the engineer Isambard Kingdom Brunel.

(British engineer ISAMBARD KINGDOM BRUNEL (1806–1859) built twenty-five railway lines, over a hundred bridges, including five suspension bridges, eight pier-and-dock systems, three ships and a pre-fabricated army field hospital.)

Medway is a Unitary Authority based on the North Kent coast in the heart of the Thames Gateway regeneration area. It is the largest conurbation outside of London in the South East of England, comprising the towns of Strood, Rochester, Chatham, Gillingham and Rainham, as well as a large rural peninsula. We benefit from excellent connectivity to London and Europe, which is assisted by high-speed rail links and access to major international airports in under one hour. Quality business space and a highly skilled workforce have made Medway a destination of choice for new businesses.

Medway comprises a population of over 250,000 and 13,000 businesses producing a local economy worth more than £2.8billion per year. Medway Council's Economic Development Team have worked hard with the engineering and manufacturing businesses to produce a vibrant sector that employs 11% of the local workforce. This is complimented by the Universities at Medway project, which now boasts four Universities and a brand new higher education college facility to provide essential skills for the future.

I am delighted to have had the opportunity to sponsor 'Made in Medway 2', which showcases the diverse range of engineering and manufacturing businesses in Medway. Many of these businesses operate in niche markets working closely with their customers to produce high quality products. What is evident from the businesses featured is the convergence of high quality engineering coupled with leading edge, creative design. I have the greatest respect for all these businesses, which have demonstrated vision, adaptability and business stamina to respond to ever changing economic conditions.

Medway Council is committed to supporting new businesses producing highly advanced products and services at the leading edge of technological development. We are the principle investor of the Medway Innovation Centre, which is a fundamental component of our strategy to provide state-of-the-art business facilities for the future.

Cllr. Jane Chitty,
Portfolio Holder for Strategic Development and Economic Growth,
Medway Council

It is with great pride that I write this foreword to the 'Made in Medway 2' book, showcasing the world-class, diverse range of manufacturing, engineering and specialist niche companies in Medway, England, UK.

Exporting globally from the UK to Europe, the Southern Hemispheres and the Far East; these companies have adapted in an ever changing (sometimes harsh) economic climate and they have demonstrated agility through adaptability and utilisation of their specialist, fine tuned niche skills in order to successfully keep manufacturing alive in Medway.

Companies featured include an impressive range of engineers, designers, furniture makers, jewellers, shirtmakers, leather manufacturers and even a Medway brewery. At the heart of these successful enterprises are the people of Medway and the creative and business community who contribute their talents to business and society prosperity.

Everyday in my professional role, I recognise how the University for the Creative Arts (UCA) community of professional practitioners and students extend their influence locally and globally through creative problem solving and innovation. This 'Made in Medway 2' book is a shared vision of Steve and Bianca who have engaged and collaborated with key Medway stakeholders to present us with even more best-kept secrets and hidden gems than in the first edition of 'Made in Medway'.

As Medway Culture Partnership Chair I have another best-kept secret to share – which is the incredible wealth of talent of the creative professionals living and working in Medway. People in our community who volunteer hours and expertise to contribute to the emerging strategic direction of culture, integrated with the regeneration plans of Medway. Their influence in shaping the strategy and building upon the rich heritage of Medway is aspirational with a commitment to deliver a robust plan to realise the potential of the area.

The talent featured in 'Made in Medway 2' is evidence of local vibrant inclusive collaborations, leadership and resources. This shared belief and resilience thrives and contributes to the well-being of the Medway community and support for economic success.

Dianne Taylor BA(Hons), H.Dip (Slade), PGCE, FRSA
Pro Vice-Chancellor and Executive Dean
University for the Creative Arts

Medway Culture Partnership Chair

Where can you go to get...
Precision engineering, vacuum forming gears, sprockets, pulleys, flight-deck systems vehicle power management systems, pilot sticks, gold & diamond encrusted mobile phones, silverware trophies, pure herbal medicines, gas mixers, devices to measure eye movements, image analysers, industrial filters, luxury soft furnishings, presentation plaques, shrink wrapped sleeves, bespoke kitchen machinery, architectural handrails luxury hand finished leather, water tanks security cases, tracking systems, bespoke handmade furniture, jubilee hose clips hydraulic cylinders, piers, floating homes pontoons, thermoset injection moulding gas analysers, natural fibre ropes and yarns air filtration systems, architectural models custom paintwork, 'friggin in the riggin' ale in ear monitors, hearing aids, bespoke shirts tilt wheelchairs, pipe clips, jewellery and architectural water fountains..?   Medway!

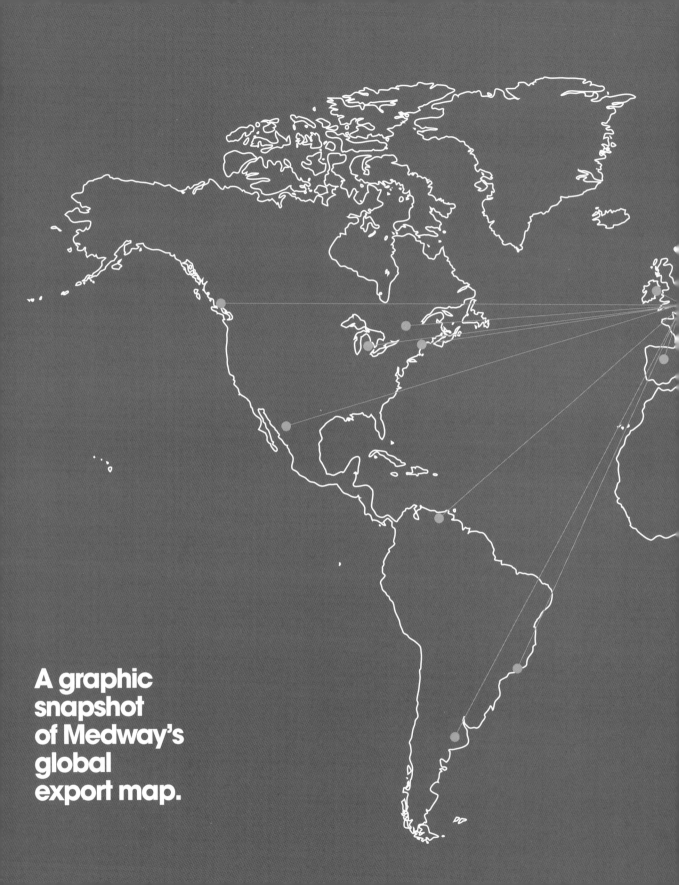

**A graphic
snapshot
of Medway's
global
export map.**

Master Ropemakers

'Be honest in your business dealings.'

Describe yourself in three words.
Businessman, local politician.

Who or what inspires you?
The achievement of success through hard work.

What can't you live without?
Holidays.

Best thing about Medway?
It's in a good location.

Your most unusual commission?
Making a hangman's noose for the film industry.

What puts a smile on your face?
Listening to and playing music (rock 'n' roll).

Who do you admire most?
Richard Branson, for being a successful entrepreneur.

What is the best piece of advice you've ever received?
Cash is king.

Your philosophy in a nutshell?
Be honest in your business dealings …

Master Ropemakers Ltd is the oldest rope manufacturer in the UK, based in the Ropery at the Historic Dockyard (rope was manufactured here for Admiral Nelson's HMS *Victory* and has been produced here since 1618). In fact, the Historic Dockyard is now on the government's shortlist of potential World Heritage Sites. The four buildings of the Ropery form one of the finest integrated groups of 18th-century manufacturing buildings in Britain. The main building, the Double Ropehouse, was built during the Napoleonic Wars to house the spinning, closing and laying processes. A historic gem, it contains the last remaining traditional working ropewalk from the Age of Sail to survive anywhere in the world.

The Ropery has been operated by the Master Ropemakers for over twenty years. Managing Director Colin Parr took over the running of the site in 1984, when the Royal Navy docks closed. Originally from Lancashire, his background lies in the accountancy and manufacturing industries. There are currently eight people working for the company. In terms of approach, they utilise specialist skills and craftsmanship; machinery dating back to the 1800s is still used. However, these techniques are combined with contemporary methods in order to adapt and stay ahead of their competitors. Because the ropewalk is 311 metres long (approximately a quarter of a mile), the employees use bicycles as a means of transport to manoeuvre back and forth!

Today the company produces rope and yarn commercially and specialises in the supply and manufacture of both natural (sisal, manila, hemp and coir) and synthetic fibres (nylon, polyester and polypropylene). Its unique facilities comprise both assured to BS EN 9000 and aims to offer customers a high level of service, product quality and flexibility. With an extensive client base (both in the UK and Europe) Master Ropemakers continues to make rope that is used aboard the world's finest sailing ships. It supplies a diverse range of sectors, including the boating industry, commercial marine, cruise ships, film industry, Ministry of Defence, rebuild and restoration of historical ships and industrial divisions.

The Ropery buildings themselves are often used as a film location. The BBC used the Tarred Yarn Store as the workhouse in its 2007 adaptation of *Oliver Twist*. Visitors can also join tours of the quarter-mile long Ropehouse and view its craftsmen at work.

Master Ropemakers Ltd
Colin Parr
T: +44 (0)1634 827 812
E: colin@master-ropemakers.co.uk
W: www.master-ropemakers.co.uk

Rayner & Sturges

'Don't throw your old shoes away until you have some new ones.'

Describe yourself in three words.
A quintessential Englishman.

Your most overused phrase?
Having turned left on the aeroplane,
I never wish to turn right again.

What inspires you?
To consistently improve the standard of
the finest shirts in England.

What has been your most unusual commission?
Making shirts for the late William Tallon,
'Backstairs Billy' – the late Elizabeth the
Queen Mother's Steward and Page of the
Backstairs.

Best thing about Medway?
The residential community.

The best piece of advice you have been given?
Don't throw your old shoes away until
you have some new ones.

Who do you admire most and why?
My late father suffered from polio from an
early age and consequently had to walk
with sticks for most of his life. He also lost his
mother, father and sister when he was just
eleven years old. Yet despite this he won
a scholarship to Cambridge and went
on to become a diplomat. He died aged
eighty-one, and I never heard him swear
or complain about his life once.

Your philosophy in a nutshell?
If you enjoy your work you will always look
forward to waking up the next day.

Rayner & Sturges is one of the UK's premier shirt-making businesses, supplying Savile Row and Jermyn Street, not to mention a coveted list of high-net-worth clients from across the globe.

Originally a shirt-collar factory, the business was established in 1913 by William Claude Sturges and Mr Raynor, who set up workrooms at a Victorian printworks in Brompton, Kent. Mr Raynor departed in 1930, leaving the Sturges family to grow the business. In 1962 demand for detachable collars had declined, and, in order to survive, the business changed direction, moving from collars to shirt-making.

Over the next thirty years Rayner & Sturges had to evolve further to stay in business. With companies relocating and outsourcing to the Indian Ocean or the Far East, it saw 95 per cent of its manufacturing base in the UK erode. So instead, the Sturges family adapted the business to become one of the very few manufacturers specialising in bespoke shirts (cotton, silk and linen) and special garments, building up an impressive list of stage, screen and sports star clientele.

In 2006, and four generations on, the Sturges family finally sold the business. The new owner, Robert Boyd Bowman, has worked closely with the Medway-based team, using his forty-six years of experience in the textile trade to help improve and modernise the business while maintaining its reputation for high quality and craftsmanship. With new customer service, tracking technology and sustainable policies – such as sourcing organic cotton and using hybrid cars – in place, the company is preparing for a prosperous future. It currently has forty-two employees. Over the next few years expansion of the customer base in the UK, USA, Japan, China and Europe is top of Mr Boyd Bowman's agenda as he sets about cutting the quintessentially English business the global profile it deserves.

Raynor & Sturges
Robert Boyd Bowman
T: +44 (0)1634 843 181
E: admin@raynersturges.com
W: www.raynersturges.co.uk

'The process of squirting impression material into Madonna's ears generated an interesting response!'

Describe yourself in three words.
Loyal, honest, dedicated.

What is your earliest memory?
Finding a hedgehog in the garage and getting a cushion and blanket to keep it warm – I was only three!

What can't you live without?
My family. Without their love and support my life would be meaningless.

What has been your most unusual commission?
I was asked to take impressions of Madonna's ears to enable us to manufacture some miniature in-ear monitors for the film *Evita*. The process of squirting impression material into Madonna's ears generated an interesting response!

Who do you admire most and why?
My father. His utmost and endless dedication to his family, his business and to all around him is a true inspiration to me.

Best thing about Medway?
The history.

What in your opinion will be the 'next big thing'?
We plan to expand our manufacturing in the UK, and this means creating more employment opportunities in Medway.

What is your philosophy in a nutshell?
Be happy, be honest, work hard and play harder.

When Jay Choudhry OBE set up his hearing-products business back in 1976 he never dreamt it would become an award-winning success story with a long list of superstar clients. But that is exactly what he and his son Baz have managed to achieve.

After ten years working for a large multinational electronics firm, Mr Choudhry decided to go it alone, and Puretone was founded thirty-two years ago. Originally repairing and designing hearing aids from his Tonbridge living-room, Puretone quickly took off and moved to larger premises in the town before moving to the Medway City Estate in Rochester in 1987. But it was when his son Baz joined the company that things really started to take shape. With a background in computing and management, Baz brought a fresh perspective, adding a complete range of accessories, batteries and earmoulds and a secure online ordering facility to the core hearing-aid repair, design and manufacture business.

He also helped establish Puretone as one of the world's leading suppliers of custom-made devices for top performers such as Kylie Minogue, Madonna, Robbie Williams and George Michael, who use them both for in-ear monitoring and noise protection. The earpieces are also used extensively by TV presenters, sound engineers and the police service and are just one of a complete range of hearing instruments manufactured at the Rochester facility, including what is possibly the smallest hearing instrument in the world today – the Ultra CIC 2010.

Today Puretone is one of the UK's premier manufacturers of quality hearing aids, tinnitus devices and faceplate kits, exporting products to over ninety-two countries worldwide and employing forty-five staff. It has gathered an impressive portfolio of awards and accreditations over the past thirty years, including the prestigious Queen's Award for Export Achievement, Investors in People and Medway Company of the Year (2007). With Jay having recently retired, Baz has taken up the reins as Managing Director and is ready to steer his award-winning business to yet further success.

Puretone
Baz Choudhry
T: +44 (0)1634 719 427
E: baz@puretone.net
W: www.puretone.net

BAE Systems

'Customer first, embrace the opportunities, enthuse with your team and anything is possible.'

Describe what you do.
I am the UK MD of the Platform Solutions business within BAE Systems and Vice-President of our global Defence Avionics business. I'm responsible for the care and development of 1,600+ people at the Rochester site and for successful delivery of our Defence Avionics Systems from our five sites in the UK and USA.

What is your background?
I trained as an electronic engineer, spending seventeen years leading programmes and businesses in the space sector.

Best thing about Medway?
Medway has always had a pool of skilled labour. Communications are good, with the motorway and airports in reasonable proximity. We have good support from local universities and are a sponsor of the Medway Innovation Centre.

What puts a smile on your face?
The letters we get from airmen and women who describe how our products have helped save lives.

The best piece of advice you've been given?
Life is about the journey, enjoy the view.

What, in your opinion, will be the 'next big thing'?
Green issues. Hybrid and fuel-efficient aircraft are hugely important. In a global world 'telepresence' will also become important over the next few years.

Your philosophy in a nutshell?
Customer first, embrace the opportunities, enthuse with your team and anything is possible.

As an international conglomerate, BAE Systems needs little introduction! In fact, it will celebrate a hundred years of supplying avionic equipment in 2009. Its Rochester site is concerned with the research, design, development and production of high-technology products. There are approximately 1,700 employees involved in all aspects of the business. However, they also employ significant staff in support functions such as works engineering, human resources, catering and security.

The production volumes at Rochester are small, but quality and reliability are paramount in the extremely demanding environment in which the products operate. In addition, these products must have a long life (sometimes as long as thirty years) and be supportable over that time. Historically the majority of products have been for the global military-aerospace customer. Items include flight controls, displays and advanced sticks and throttles. However, significant business has been acquired for commercial aerospace, notably flight controls and head-up displays for civil transports.

BAE Systems is in the business of precision electronic engineering at its highest level. In electronics the company uses the most advanced circuit devices and display devices. The design of mechanical assemblies to meet harsh environmental conditions and operational stress requires knowledge and capability in many exotic materials. Lightweight alloys, metals and advanced carbon-fibre materials are vital to reduce weight and yet provide strength in products, particularly head-mounted displays. Some of these materials and fabrication techniques have been derived in collaboration with the McLaren Formula 1 racing team.

In terms of sustainable policies, the BAE Systems Group President has coined the strategy 'Global, Green and Growing'. The company is one of the world's largest providers of hybrid electric systems for buses, which reduce carbon emissions and make them more fuel efficient.

BAE Systems creates over a hundred new inventions every year for customers in over a hundred countries. Their client base is global, serving the major aerospace sectors, particularly in the US, UK, France, Germany, Italy, Middle East and the Far East. The Company has won fifteen Queen's Awards since 1968, seven of which have been for export and the remainder for technology. The last Queen's Award was in 2002 for innovation in helmet-mounted displays. There have also been numerous awards from suppliers for quality and safety and personnel awards from professional institutions.

BAE Systems
Andy Start, Rochester Site Executive
T: +44 (0)1634 844 400
E: ps.communications3@baesystems.com
W: www. baesystems.com

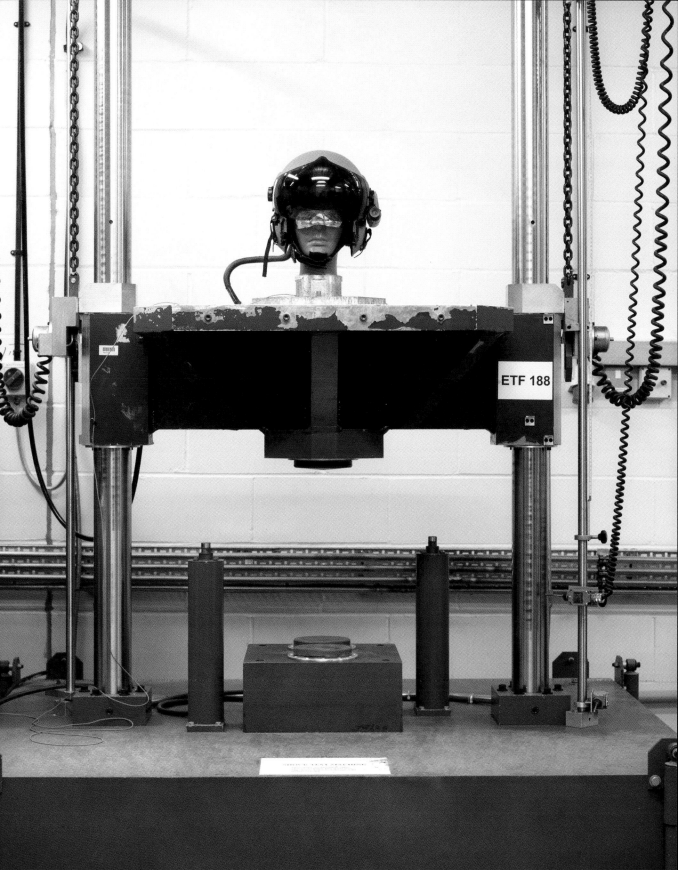

ETF 188

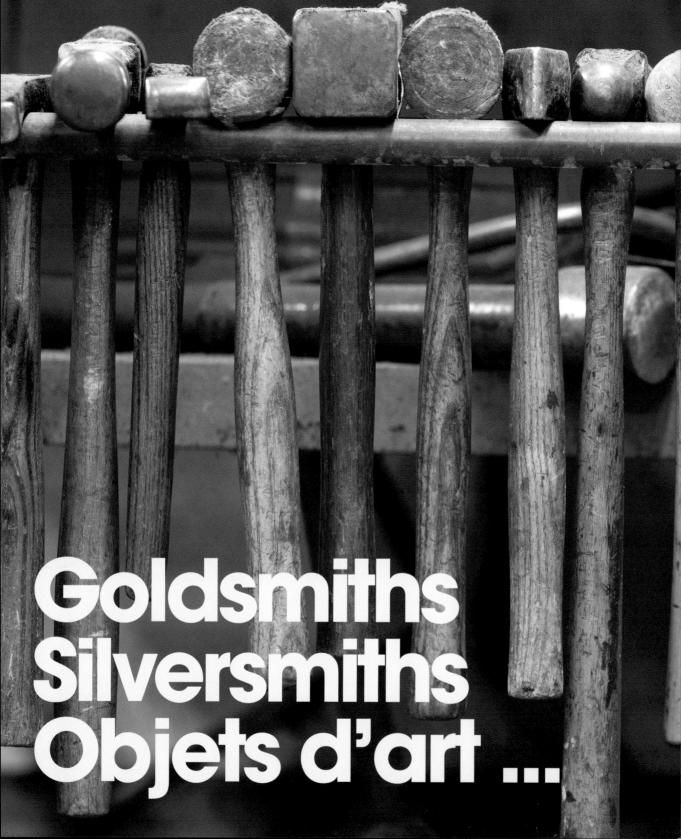

Goldsmiths
Silversmiths
Objets d'art ...

Sarena Manufacturing

'It's great to have the assistance of organisations like the Manufacturing Advisory Service (MAS) to help us maintain our competitive edge.'

Describe yourself in three words.
My dad's daughter.

Who or what inspires you?
Seeing the positive effects of change.

Best thing about Medway?
Being a university town there is a huge pool of knowledge on our doorstep. I'd encourage any business to engage with their local university – it's a win-win-win situation for the company, the student and the university.

What do you consider to be your greatest achievement?
Getting full marks in a spelling test when I was aged seven. All the rest has built from that moment.

Your philosophy in a nutshell?
If things go wrong, find the cause and correct it, rather than finding the person and blaming them.

Has the manufacturing industry changed since you've been in business?
British manufacturing is constantly under pressure from imports. We need to be able to offer something different – service, new products, green initiatives – and constantly look at improvements. It's great to have the assistance of organisations like the Manufacturing Advisory Service to help us maintain our competitive edge.

What in your opinion will be the 'next big thing'?
The resurgence of British manufacturing as transport costs make imports too expensive (hopefully!).

The best piece of advice you've been given?
Nil illegitimus carborundum …

Sarena Manufacturing was founded in 1958 as a glass-fibre moulding company producing a range of products for the UK market. It relocated to Medway in 1988 from Bow, East London, and today Sarena is the longest-established privately owned manufacturer in its field. It serves the utilities and building-services industries with glass-reinforced plastics such as fibreglass tanks for the storage and distribution of water.

Suzanne Wood is the General Manager. Her role is to ensure the company continues to improve, and to achieve this she has to be proficient in all aspects of the business. For many, this would be quite a daunting prospect. But Suzanne has a vast and varied background, including running a tomato nursery, lecturing in business management and project management at a brand-design company.

A proud supporter of British manufacturing, Suzanne believes that if British companies are to survive the pressure from imports they need to be able to offer something different. At Sarena she is addressing this by focusing on five key areas: improved service; customisation; new products; constant review and improvement of productivity; and exploring more sustainable, environmentally friendly business practices.

From the outset the company has supplied products to the water industry and so is more aware than most of what a precious a commodity it is. Water conservation is just one of the environmental issues Suzanne and her team have on their agenda. The company is currently working towards the ISO 14001 standard and is looking at ways of reducing waste, recycling, sourcing sustainable raw materials and managing energy usage effectively. It's an ongoing project that staff at all levels of the business are proud to be involved in. Suzanne's attention to detail as General Manager is clearly paying dividends; Sarena were shortlisted for the Kent Business Awards 2007 for excellence in training and development.

Water tanks and housing products aren't the only things that Sarena manufactures. The company has worked on many different commissions, including creating the archway at Dickens World that emulates a Victorian sewer! Diversification and working on ever more challenging projects is something that Sarena is keen to explore. While the water industry will always remain at the company's core, the Sarena team is constantly developing new products and has other sectors firmly in their sights for the future.

Sarena Manufacturing Limited
Suzanne Wood
T: +44 (0)1634 370 887
E: suzanne@sarena.co.uk
W: www.sarena.co.uk

J and A Precision Engineering

'If you can't give it 100 per cent then don't do it.'

Describe yourself in three words.
Stubborn, fussy, reliable.

Who or what inspires you?
Deadlines.

What is your earliest memory?
Being in hospital as a child.

What puts a smile on your face?
A job well done.

What can't you live without?
Good food.

Who do you admire the most?
Efficient people, because they get the job done.

What is the best piece of advice you've been given?
If you can't give it 100 per cent then don't do it.

What do you consider to be your greatest achievement?
Surviving in business for thirty years.

Your most overused phrase?
I don't believe it!

It was 1975 when Tug Lowe, Alan Lister and John Whiting decided to go into business together. They'd been working together at another firm but decided they could do better themselves, and as a result J and A Precision Engineering was born. Tug is the only remaining founder at the company but continues to insist on the same high standards that were so important to the three friends from the outset.

In the early days the company mainly picked up subcontracted work. Over time it has built a strong reputation for delivering quality and consistency and today provides services such as CNC turning and milling, precision assembly, prototype design and general precision engineering direct to customers from across the UK. For example, it counts Handrail Design, London Bearing and BACTEC International among its current customers.

BACTEC International specialises in bomb-disposal probes, travelling all over the world clearing landmines and unexploded bombs. J and A Precision Engineering makes the probes used by BACTEC to detonate these unexploded ordnances and has recently delivered probes to help check the Olympic sites for London 2012. This specialist field is incredibly tough, and J and A Precision Engineering are at the forefront of its research and technology. In fact, the company has just developed a slimmer probe, which has been declared successful after trials abroad.

Operating in specialist sectors has helped J and A Precision Engineering to carve out a niche, thus enabling the company to go from strength to strength. As well as delivering high-quality work, growth has been, and always will be, its primary focus. J and A is already planning its next expansion – the company is moving to new and more modern premises in early 2009, which it hopes will improve productivity. It looks like it will be a busy year ahead for the company, but one thing's for sure: its precision engineering team will be giving it at least 100 per cent!

J and A Precision Engineering
Tug Lowe
T: +44 (0)1634 406727
E: mail@jandaprecisioneng.co.uk
W: www.jandaprecisioneng.co.uk

The Nelson Brewing Company

'We have no waste. Hops get dug into allotments as compost and the malt remains go to farmers, used in food for their animals.'

Describe yourself in three words.
Loyal, kind, determined.

Who or what inspires you?
Ian Botham – he performed at a top sporting level and still managed to enjoy himself. His greatest friend Viv Richards was also his greatest adversary.

Best thing about Medway?
A hot, sunny day in the dockyard.

What materials do you specialise in?
As the Stella Artois advert said, there's five: water, malt, barley, hops and yeast.

Does your business employ any green or sustainable policies?
We have no waste, hops get dug into allotments as compost and the malt remains go to farmers, used in food for their animals.

Your earliest memory?
I had a Camberwick Green fort, but because I was so horrible and naughty my mum burnt it and made me watch. I was traumatized for years …

The best piece of advice you've been given?
Always treat people as you wish to be treated yourself.

What do you consider to be your greatest achievement?
Winning the best Kentish beer after three months of running the company with Pieces of Eight.

Has the manufacturing industry changed since you've been in business?
Prices of raw materials have increased – malt by 20 per cent – yet you can't increase customers' prices.

Situated in Chatham's Historic Dockyard is Piers MacDonald, the proud owner of the Nelson Brewery and purveyor of fine Kentish ale. Originally from Maidstone, Piers describes himself as 'passionate about brewing real ale' – he's well placed to make this claim, having run pubs for twenty years. When the smoking ban came into effect, he decided to get out of the pub-licensing industry, fearing it would damage trade. He clearly made the right decision. Sales of his bottled beer have risen from 5 to more than 25 per cent of the company's turnover, indicating that more people are drinking at home than ever before.

Piers bought the Nelson Brewery in July 2006. The company is named after Admiral Horatio Nelson, whose flagship, the *Victory*, was built in the dockyard. It's tucked away inside an atmospheric location; the building dates back to the 1850s and was originally the Dockyard's boiler house. There are currently five people working for the company, all with considerable expertise in the brewing industry. They use five different types of Kentish hops in the manufacturing process.

The company is a five-barrel plant, with the capacity to brew up to 100 barrels a week. It takes approximately eight hours to brew a beer, of which there are usually eleven or twelve different types on offer, including stout. All the ales have nautical-themed names to acknowledge the surroundings in which they are brewed. Piers comes up with such naval-inspired gems as Friggin in the Riggin (their bestseller) and Nelson's Blood. Special commemorative beers are also on the agenda – the Task Force beer was created in conjunction with the Falklands Veterans' Foundation to mark the twenty-fifth anniversary of that conflict.

The brewery labels and bottles every one of its beers in-house. This is, incidentally, done by hand, not on a production line. Although it's a time consuming operation this hands-on approach is refreshing – it saves on their carbon footprint and ensures complete quality control.

Piers is justifiably proud of the company's success – he had only been running the Nelson Brewery for three months when they won the 2006 Taste of Kent Award for their Pieces of Eight ale. They have a strong client base across the south-east of England, including London, and also sell at farmers' markets. Visitors to the brewery are always welcome. The company offers tours where you can view the brewing process, smell the aromatic hops and relax with a refreshing pint at their bar afterwards.

Nelson Brewery
Piers MacDonald
T: +44(0)1634 832 828
E: sales@nelsonbrewingcompany.co.uk
W: www.nelsonbrewingcompany.co.uk

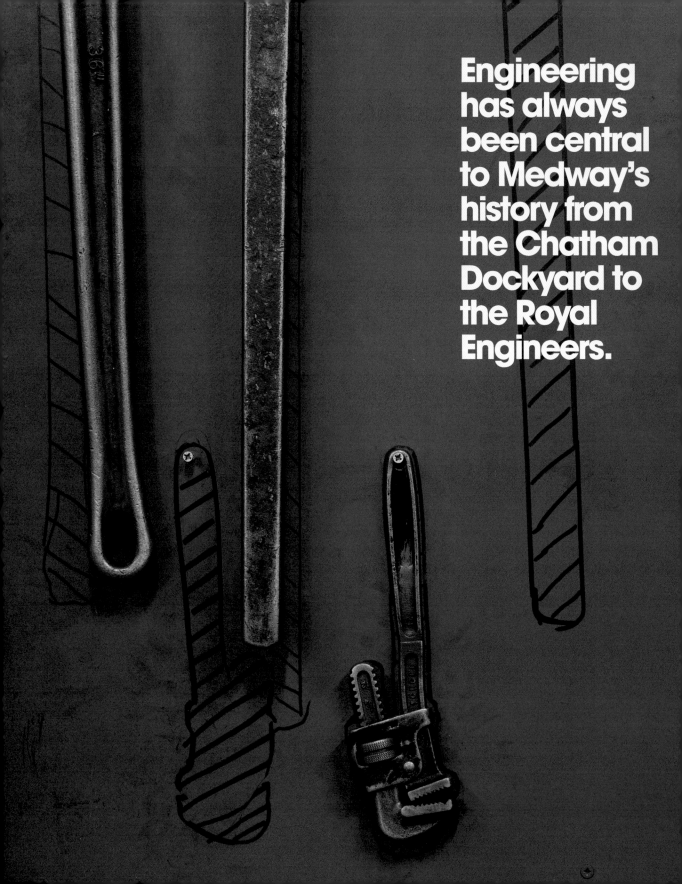

Engineering has always been central to Medway's history from the Chatham Dockyard to the Royal Engineers.

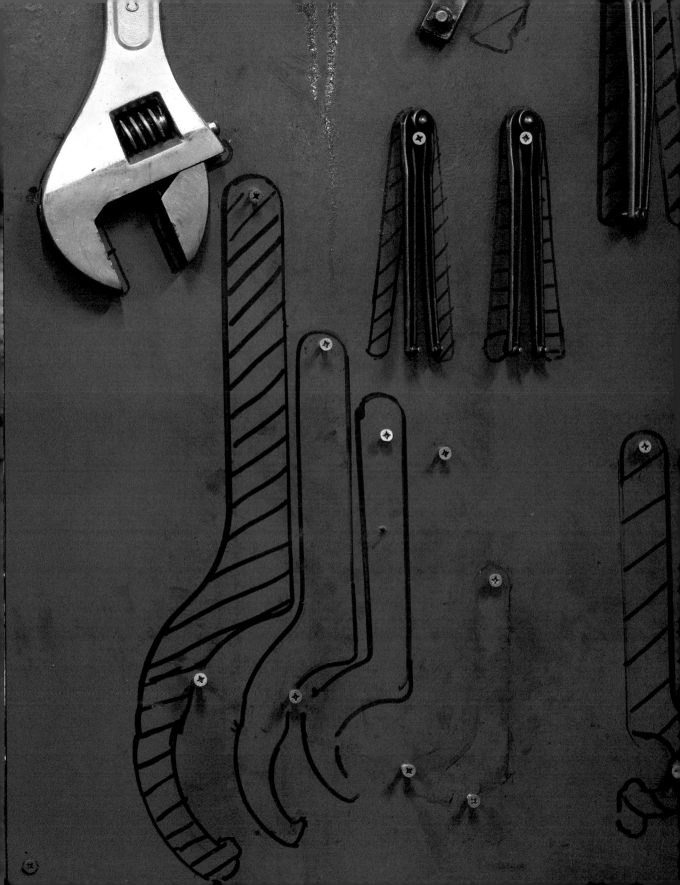

Hutchfield Furniture

'Tough times don't last, but tough people do.'

Describe yourself in three words.
Concerned about everything.

What puts a smile on your face?
Clients saying thank you.

Best thing about Medway?
It has an excellent transport infrastructure and lots of skills still surviving from the ship-building industries. There is also a good array of local suppliers.

What do you consider to be your greatest achievement?
Helping create a skilled, coherent and conscientious workforce.

Your earliest memory?
Falling into brambles and stinging nettles as a child.

What can't you live without?
My family, dog, pipe, pencil, good wine and friends …

Who do you admire most?
Spike Milligan. His humour brought laughter to millions, while struggling with himself.

The best piece of advice you've been given?
Tough times don't last, but tough people do.

Your most unusual commission?
We made a library table for Magdalen College, Oxford, using a fallen oak tree from the college quadrangle. However, the inside was rotten, so it proved to be rather challenging!

What in your opinion will be the 'next big thing'?
The transfer of economic power from the West to the East.

As manufacturers, designers and specialists in veneering, Hutchfield Furniture works to a broad remit while retaining impeccable standards of craftsmanship, offering a bespoke-furniture service from concept to completion with an emphasis on high-end design. Richard Hutchfield established the company in 1991 and has been manufacturing in Medway ever since. Originally from Castle Cary in Somerset, he trained at Somerset College of Art and the London College of Furniture, where he established Cathedra (a made-to-order furniture company) with four college friends. Cathedra produced a considerable number of projects in the 1980s for large financial institutions, and this business expertise was transferred across to Hutchfield Furniture.

There are currently ten people working for the company. Paddy the cocker spaniel is their eleventh honorary employee and has been coming to work with Richard every day for the last seven and a half years! The client base encompasses the commercial, retail and public sectors as well as institutions such as Oxford University. The company also undertakes specialist domestic projects from time to time – notably for Roman Abramovich, the Russian billionaire and owner of Chelsea Football Club, who commissioned furniture for his estate and private yacht.

Veneering is one of the firm's specialities. The makers work with an incredible array of exotic woods such as bubinga, strawberry and ebony as well as the traditional cherry, maple and walnut. In terms of sustainability, the company purchases timber products certified by the Forestry Stewardship Council and uses materials from well-managed forests. The company also recycles as much as possible. Although timber-based materials are used frequently, Hutchfield Furniture can work with glass, foam, MDF, PVC, multimedia, stainless steel and stone. Richard has seen the manufacturing industry change considerably since he's been in business. CAD has enabled structures, which were not possible before. Similarly, computer numerically controlled machines now provide more precision, efficiency and consistency. As a result, he has had to learn, borrow and invest in order to remain successful through these technological changes.

Clients include the BBC, Roman Abramovich, Oxford University, the Royal Household and, more recently, Manchester Airport, which commissioned Hutchfield Furniture to develop a unique fluid seating system for its departure lounge. There are also customers in Ireland, Frankfurt, Geneva, Luxembourg, Moscow and Paris. The company has won numerous awards, including the Carpenters Award and the Medway Partners for Growth Award. Richard is also a Churchill Fellow.

Hutchfield Furniture Ltd
Richard Hutchfield
T: +44 (0)1634 819 256
E: richard@hutchfield-furniture.co.uk

'The best thing about Medway is the large number of small companies that can do or make almost anything.'

Describe yourself in three words.
Practical, cantankerous, bald.

Best thing about Medway?
The large number of small companies that can do or make almost anything. Whatever we need, there seems to be someone in a small unit around the corner who can do it at short notice.

What has been your most unusual commission?
I once had a go at some animatronics. We needed a human head for an exhibition, so I bought a plastic skull (the type used to teach medical students) and repositioned two table-football balls as eyes. I then constructed elaborate motor-and-pulley systems to drive them around inside the skull. It was fun but more difficult than I imagined!

What can't you live without?
The internet, coffee, long hot baths and a large supply of lined A4 writing paper.

The best piece of advice you've been given?
If you are having trouble deciding between two things it probably doesn't matter much which one you choose.

Does your business employ any green policies?
As a business we strive for a paperless office and diligently recycle. Electronics, in general, has become more green with the use of lead-free components and the drive to reduce power consumption in electronic equipment in general.

Cambridge Research Systems (CRS) was originally formed in 1996 as a partnership between John Robson, a distinguished vision scientist at Cambridge University, and his son Tom Robson, an engineer who also graduated from Cambridge. By using the latest cutting-edge technologies they've developed a number of standard laboratory techniques, providing customers with the right tools to help research any aspect of sight, seeing or vision. CRS has developed equipment to stimulate the visual cortex, devices to measure eye movements and image-analysers used to measure flashing images in broadcast TV programmes that might induce epileptic seizures.

Although Tom Robson is CEO of the company, he remains, first and foremost, an engineer. He has a keen interest in cutting-edge technology and has built a world-class team of product-development engineers, which he leads with an inventive solutions-oriented approach. Tom's job is to talk to customers, mostly in the bioscience field, and distil their requirements into a design for a manufacturable product. Sometimes it works the other way round; long-term customers come to CRS with the results of promising research that could have a big impact if only it were turned into something a patient or hospital could buy.

Most of CRS's work involves electronics and computers, which have changed daily for the last forty years. In Tom's opinion, this is what makes the industry so exciting. Adapting and keeping ahead is almost a full-time occupation for the CRS team, and building sophisticated scientific equipment on a small scale becomes harder as customers become used to the incredible technology found on most modern consumer goods.

But with twenty-three years under its belt, the company still manages to keep one step ahead. Its clients are global, with its biggest markets being the UK, USA and Japan. Currently most equipment the company manufactures is used for academic research in universities and hospitals, but it's embarking on some mainstream products for the future. One product that has really taken off is the Harding Flash and Patter Analyser, which was shortlisted as a finalist for a Royal Television Award. The product protects television viewers from epileptic seizures caused by flashing images, and the CRS team is justifiably proud that it's now used throughout the UK and Japan.

Cambridge Research Systems Ltd
Tom Robson
T: +44 (0)1634 720 707
E: enquiries@crsltd.com
W: www.crsltd.com

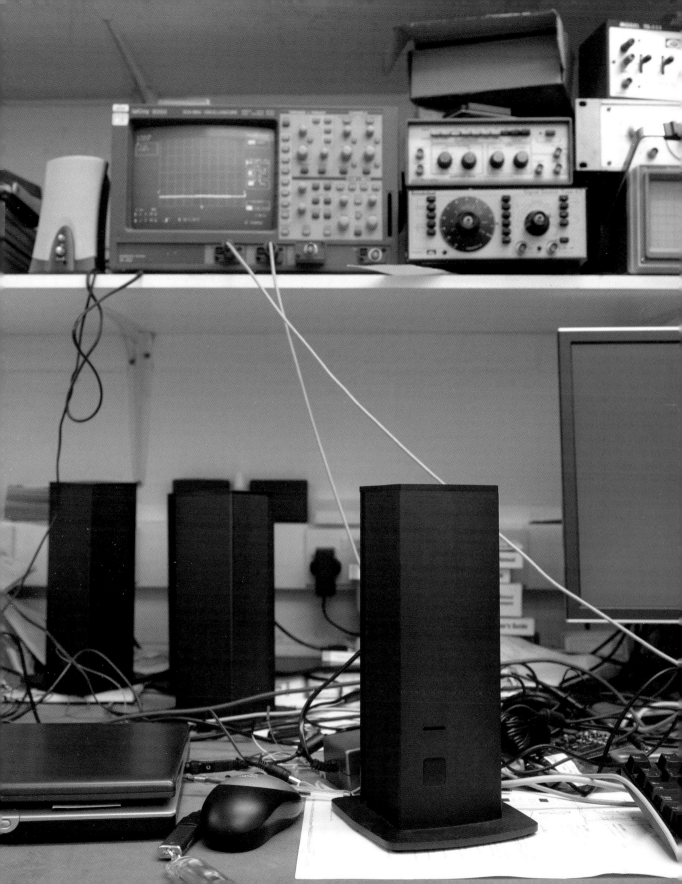

HDH Security Systems

'The wheel wasn't invented by cutting too many corners.'

Describe yourself in three words.
Content, hardworking, ambitious.

Best thing about Medway?
It's local to London and Dover and gives us easy access to European commerce.

What is your background?
Electronics learnt at the Merchant Navy officers' college HMS *Worcester* in Greenhithe, Kent.

What inspires you?
My wife, children and the need to succeed.

Does your business employ any green or sustainable policies?
Yes, we recycle batteries and use rechargeable where possible. We also recycle paper and tin.

What puts a smile on your face?
Happy people.

What is your earliest memory?
Lying in my cot when I was about one. I can still remember the pattern on the blanket.

The worst job you've ever done?
Playing piano at pantomime and enduring two matinee's per day, six days a week!

What is the best piece of advice you've been given?
Work hard to play hard and treat others how you would like to be treated.

Who do you admire most and why?
Dyson, Branson and Trevor Baylis because they are inventive and entrepreneurial.

Your most overused phrases?
It's not rocket science.

Your philosophy in a nutshell
The wheel wasn't invented by cutting too many corners.

When Michael Hewitt first set up HDH Security Systems in 1997 his primary goal was to earn enough money to fund the research and development work he was undertaking with Kent University. Michael wanted to develop new products, and the income from the company would enable him to achieve that. But the company began to do well, and so he turned his focus to building the business to what it is today.

Chatham-based HDH Security Systems designs and manufactures specialist security equipment for the retail, cash-in-transit and banking industries. Its niche products range from security cases to special cash-in-transit smoke-dye systems that enable the police to track stolen goods and recover them.

The company offers a unique level of asset protection to its customers, and this is reflected in its broad client base of commercial and industrial clients throughout the UK and Europe. This looks set to expand with the company receiving interest from clients in Kenya, Nigeria and Uganda. Examples of some the HDH's most recent clients include Historic Royal Palaces, Securicor, Brinks UK, the Post Office and HM Prison Service.

But by far the most unusual job Mike and his team of five have worked on was fitting a tracking system to tree roots! Valuable saplings were being stolen in large quantities from a farm, and HDH Security Systems was called in to install a tracking system to trap the thief. The products Mike and his team have developed have won them awards and widespread recognition, including a DTI Smart Award, when they won £45,000 to develop a new security-ink-dispensing system, and being shortlisted for the 2008 International Transmanche Business Awards.

HDH Security Systems
Michael Hewitt
T: +44 (0)1634 302 616
E: hdhss@aol.com
W: www.hdhss.com

Diverse markets such as the Microelectronic, Pharmaceutical, Research, Health, Decontamination, Defence and Nuclear industries.

RKR Engineering

'Believe in yourself and everything becomes possible.'

Describe yourself in three words.
Positive, confident, dedicated.

What is the best piece of advice you've been given?
Believe in yourself and everything becomes possible.

What puts a smile on your face?
Achievement.

Who inspires you?
My wife.

Best thing about Medway?
The regeneration of the area and the people that live here.

Who do you admire most and why?
My father, because he has always encouraged me to do my best.

What do you consider to be your greatest achievement?
Building my OWN purpose-built factory.

What are your most overused phrases?
Not a problem.

What is your philosophy in a nutshell?
Work hard and everything's achievable.

Raj Ram has worked in manufacturing engineering all his life. His love of product development and desire to prove that his products and ideas could work drove him to set up his own business.

Originally from West Ham, he set up RKR Engineering in Rochester in 1996 and, with several skilled workers from his old company and a selection of manual lathes, began by securing general machining work. The support of his bank and accountant, and the receipt of a council grant, helped drive him forward. Before long he had expanded the business, establishing a second site in Essex to help cope with demand.

The company specialises in all types of metal, wood and plastics and can manufacture in-house up to an impressive 5 tonnes. With the biggest vertical milling machine in Kent, RKR Engineering delivers precision engineering on a huge scale to clients in a multitude of sectors, manufacturing anything from drill bits to components to power stations and cranes.

Winning large-scale contracts with clients such as EDF Energy has driven the need for RKR Engineering to further expand over the past year, quadrupling its warehouse workspace to cope with demand. It is also in the process of moving its Essex premises to Medway to consolidate its operations.

So what's the key to the company's success? According to Raj it's a combination of a positive approach, self-belief, hard work and good team spirit. All twenty employees work together to deliver on orders, Raj included. Investment in technology has also helped improve the company's capabilities, and this is something that will continue into the future. Raj believes in his staff, his company and their collective ability to overcome any obstacle. It's this constant positive attitude that he believes will lead them on to continued success.

RKR Engineering
Mr Raj Ram
T: +44 (0)1634 723 565
E: r.k.r.eng@btconnect.com

Emery Etchings

'I'm determined to prove there is such a thing as a reliable, high-quality supplier who can be trusted.'

Describe yourself in three words.
Honest, passionate, biker.

Who or what inspires you?
I'm determined to prove there is such a thing as a reliable, high-quality supplier who can be trusted.

Best thing about Medway?
Its location and prospects for a bright future.

What puts a smile on your face?
When people see what we do, and customers wonder how we do it.

Who do you admire most and why?
Nelson Mandela for his conviction and Richard Branson for his business acumen.

Your most overused phrases?
Focus, focus, focus; and keep a tight rein on the paper trail.

What can't you live without?
My health and enthusiasm.

What do you consider to be your greatest achievement?
Creating employment and developing staff for future success.

Your philosophy in a nutshell?
To continue supplying trade customers with high-quality products. Their name is on OUR products leaving their door; not ours. THAT is the responsibility we carry.

What in your opinion will be 'the next big thing'?
The Olympics, London 2012.

Emery Etchings Ltd was first established by Brian Emery in 1997. Before this he worked for the Royal Navy and spent many years in the oil industry. Based on the Medway City Estate in Strood, the company supplies high-quality chemical-etching services and products to the engraving and sign-making trade as well as to corporate customers. Working mainly with stainless steel, bronze and polished brass, the company has manufactured hundreds of presentation plaques, many of which have been unveiled by members of the Royal Family, MPs, council officials and celebrities. It also makes corporate name plates and awards for customers both in the UK and abroad.

The chemical-etching process used by Brian and his team removes metal much quicker than any other mechanical-engraving process and, most importantly, leaves no damage to the material being used. The surface it leaves behind is also completely flat so, once painted, the finish is of a much higher quality. This process was put to the test in one of the company's most unusual commissions, a 90-by-60-centimetre stainless-steel panel with a drawing of an overview of Stourport-on-Severn etched on to it for a designer blacksmith!

The manufacturing process used by the company to achieve its high-quality products means that inevitably it's classed as a waste-chemical producer. As such, Emery Etchings is more than aware of its environmental responsibilities. It's bound by law to comply with waste regulations and is registered with the Environment Agency accordingly. The company also recycles as much as possible.

Like all manufacturing businesses, Emery Etchings has had to adapt in order to survive and prosper. With the cost of raw materials and general overheads ever increasing, the company has focused on generating as much repeat business from its customers as it can. It has achieved this by ensuring quality remains at the heart of everything it delivers. Brian believes the combination of a high-quality product service and the continued satisfaction of his customers is the key to Emery Etching's future success.

Emery Etchings
Brian Emery or Pete Spencer
T: +44 (0)1634 719 396
E: sales@emeryetchings.com
W: www.emeryetchings.com

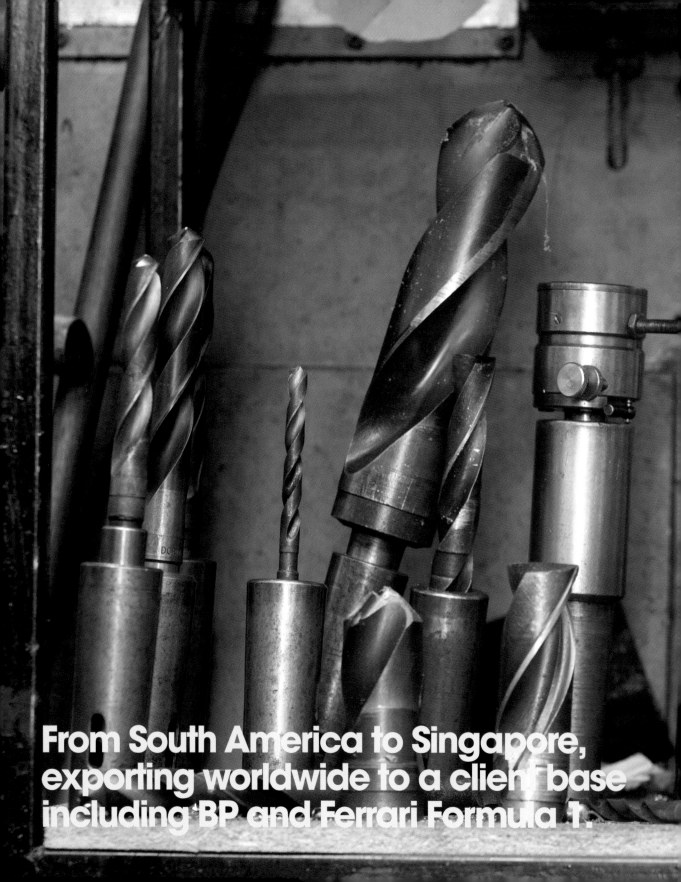

From South America to Singapore, exporting worldwide to a client base including BP and Ferrari Formula 1.

Beeby and Powell

'There is more competition from overseas. We have always been adaptable in order to survive.'

Describe yourself in three words.
Jon: Perfectionist, loyal, thoughtful.
Jim: Patient, very patient …

Best thing about Medway?
Jon: The heritage.
Jim: The river.

Your most unusual commission?
Jon: An 18-inch-tall silver-and-18-carat-gold jelly-bean machine.
Jim: A silver model of a Heidelberg printing press for the Royal Logistical Corps.

Your greatest achievement?
Jon: Winning awards for pieces I have designed and produced (awarded by my peers).
Jim: Staying in business.

Your most overused phrases?
Jon: It has to be better.
Jim: Relax …

Has the manufacturing industry changed since you've been in business?
Jim: There is more competition from overseas. We have always been adaptable in order to survive.

What in your opinion will be the 'next big thing'?
Jon: Sterling-silver models of private jets and super yachts.
Jim: Always hopeful … silverware!

Describing themselves as silversmiths who also work in gold, Jonathan Charles Beeby and James Williams Powell are, respectively, Beeby and Powell. The two business partners are versatile craftsmen specialising in silver models, trophies and table centrepieces as well as bespoke one-off pieces based on clients' specific requirements. Over the last few years they've diversified, and a wide range of commissions have been carried out, including designing jewellery and silverware, models for the British Army, a mobile telephone in gold with a diamond-encrusted key pad and torchier wall lights for the designer Jocelyn Burton.

They both studied at Medway College of Art and Design and have worked together running their business since 1990, forging a reputation for quality in design and manufacturing. Jon is originally from Portsmouth, and his background is in silversmithing; Jim is from Chatham, an ex-dockyard fitter-turner. They have many skills, between them ticking a multitude of boxes: business managers, designers, craftsmen, modelmakers, restorers and manipulators of precious metals.

They can work to any style or commission, contemporary or classic, and attention to detail is one of their specialities. Their miniature Harley Davidsons and Ferraris are impressively crafted to scale in solid sterling silver; gold-plated pieces such as their Williams Renault radio-controlled Formula 1 car are just as impressive. In terms of environmental awareness, they recycle all their silver.

Jonathan Beeby has seen the industry change dramatically in the last ten years. 'Gone are the days of factories full of craftsmen. Workshops with six people are now classed as large operations. This has forced silversmiths to take a more artistic approach, tailoring individual pieces to their clients' needs. New manufacturing processes have also come into line, that have to be utilised to keep up, live long and prosper,' he adds.

The company has a number of prestigious clients, including Asprey, Cartier, Garrards and the Royal Engineers. They also undertake restoration work for London's antiques trade. Their client base is predominantly in Medway, London and the Middle East. Over the last twenty years the duo has won twelve Goldsmith Craft Council Awards in a number of disciplines, from design and silversmithing to the manufacture of detailed scale models.

Beeby Powell
Jon Beeby and Jim Powell
T: +44(0)1634 830 764
E: mail@beebypowell.com
W: www.beebypowell.com

THE CRIMEA ARCH
Commissioned to Commemorate
the amalgamation of
12 RSME Regiment and Depot Regiment
Royal Engineers
as
1 RSME Regiment Royal Engineers
September 1994

'Our mission is to help advance medical and environmental science.'

Describe yourself in three words.
Inventive, persistent, fair.

Describe what you do.
Industrial/medical research and development plus manufacturing. We are specialists in real-time trace-gas analyser design.

What is your background?
Medical physics, electronics and bioengineering. I had twenty-five years' experience as head of a medical electronics department before starting Logan Research Ltd in 1994.

Who or what inspires you?
God's incredible designs in nature all around us.

The best piece of advice you've ever been given?
Treat people fairly, watch the cash flow like a hawk and don't rub your competitors up the wrong way as you may need them on-side later on.

Your greatest achievement?
Introducing the first fully integrated clinical nitric-oxide analyser to the world in 1994 for diagnosing and monitoring the treatment of asthmatics.

Your philosophy in a nutshell?
Our mission is to help advance medical and environmental science while being fair and considerate in all our dealings with others – even if it is not always resulting in the maximum financial reward.

Logan Research is a small but highly influential company that can take your breath away. They do it in the nicest, most productive way. But ultimately, that's what they're after: a sample of a person's breath, or more precisely, the gas he/she is breathing out. Why? So that it can be analysed for health reasons. Asthmatics are particularly grateful for this technology, but others undergoing medical tests – people with suspected liver disease or cancer, for example – can benefit too.

The company, which employs five people, designs and manufactures their analysis/screening devices in Rochester. As their name suggests, research is another important part of their work. Apart from supplying hospitals and other large medical centres, an additional market for the sort of analysers and related equipment they make is with fellow researchers doing similar types of crucial medical work in Britain and overseas.

With the emphasis in the colossal global healthcare industry increasingly on prevention rather than cure, this specialist firm has no shortage of potential patients who need to be screened. Wearing his eco-friendly cap, Ron Logan-Sinclair says that they 'take back their life-expired equipment and recycle as much as possible'.

If his next project gets off the ground, his customer base could expand further still. Ron's pioneering plan is to produce miniature versions of his gas/breath analysers, which will be used in small or remote medical centres and surgeries. And after that? Even smaller devices in the home, enabling each family member to monitor aspects of their health, simply by providing a sample of his or her breath. Yet another string to the bow of the company is that they design and manufacture environmental monitors, which can analyse air quality.

Because the units cost tens of thousands of pounds each, this is valuable and prestigious export business for the company. The Logan Research-built gas-analyser machines that come out of Rochester sell to health professionals worldwide, with customers in the USA (the University of Pittsburgh Medical Center is a client), the UK, New Zealand and Norway to name but a few.

Logan Research Ltd
Ron Logan-Sinclair
T: +44 (0)1634 294 900
E: loganres@aol.com
W: www.loganresearch.co.uk

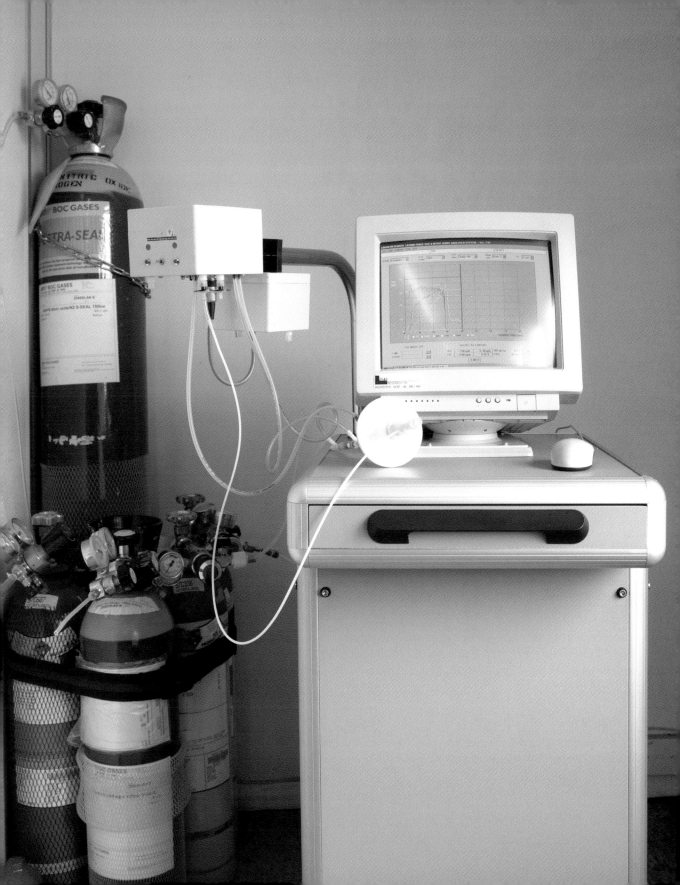

Waterman Offshore

'All the best shows have rehearsals.'

Describe yourself in three words.
Fair, approachable, friendly.

Best thing about Medway?
Medway has good transport links with an accessible motorway network.

What puts a smile on your face?
Job satisfaction.

What can't you live without?
My six-year-old English sheepdog Barney.

What is your earliest memory?
Being at school.

What do you consider to be your greatest achievement?
Running Waterman Offshore.

Your most overused phrase?
All the best shows have rehearsals.

Your philosophy in a nutshell?
Always deliver on time and to budget.

What in your opinion will be the 'next big thing'?
Retiring!

Mick Tolladay began his career with an apprenticeship in steel fabrication and welding before heading overseas for ten years to work on the oil rigs in West Africa, Singapore and Indonesia. It was his time in West Africa in particular that inspired him to start up his own business. He identified an export opportunity for the supply of fabricated steel structures and equipment. So when he arrived back in the UK in 1982 he decided to set up Waterman Offshore.

Based in Rochester, the company originally provided services to the offshore world in West Africa but has since diversified and grown to become a global industry leader throughout the offshore, engineering and fabrication industries. Today, Waterman Offshore specialises in the fabrication of steel structures, vessels, gantries, pipework and process-plant equipment. While most of its clients are global companies based predominantly in the south of the UK, the company also exports to Barbados and Ireland.

In the twenty-seven years the company has been trading, it has seen significant change. Equipment has evolved to keep up with the changes in technology and material costs have been subject to dramatic price rises. As with most other industries, the internet has also had a major impact on the way the company works, allowing it to work faster and smarter. But the team at Waterman Offshore relish change and are always on the lookout for ways to improve.

As head of the company Mick is passionate about engineering and believes in fostering new talent. He enjoys teaching his employees and young apprentices new skills, helping them learn all about engineering and providing them with the opportunity to follow a career. The company actively encourages work experience and offers work placements to schools through the Medway Education Business Partnership. In fact, they've already had six students in the business this year alone. It's the company's commitment to helping its staff continually improve that this year helped it win its Investor in People Award, an accolade that the Waterman Offshore team is justifiably proud of.

Waterman Offshore
Mick Tolladay
T: +44 (0)1634 290 519
E: enquiries@watermanoffshoreltd.co.uk
W: www.watermanoffshore.co.uk

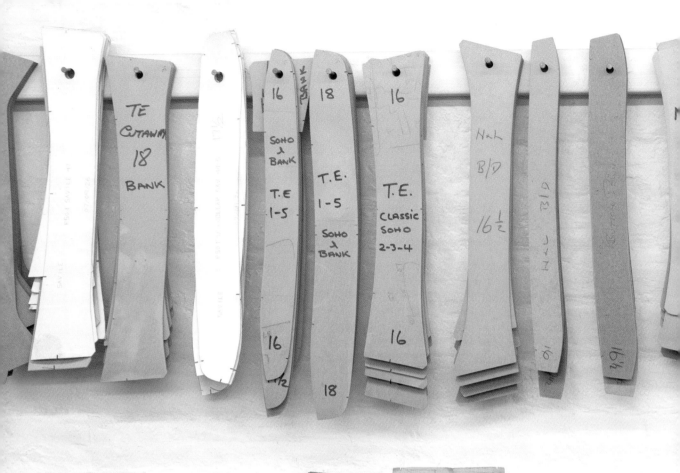

TE Cutaway 18 BANK

16

18

16

SOHO 2 BANK

T.E 1-5

T.E. 1-5

SOHO 2 BANK

T.E. CLASSIC SOHO 2-3-4

H&L B/D 16½

H&L B/D

16

16

18

TE 2 Butt 14/14½ LINING

TE 2 Butt 15/15½ LINING

TE 2 Button 16/16½

TE 3 Butt 17/17½ LINING

TE 3 Button 15/15½

TE Slim Fit 2 15-15½ 15¾

TE 15/15½ LINING

Exquisite tailoring skills, supplying shirts to the 'better end' of the trade.

ICM Plastic Moulding

'Calculated risks are a key part of an expanding business.'

Describe yourself in three words.
Enthusiastic, friendly, happy.

Best thing about Medway?
The road network, for its access to major motorways and the Continent, and the McDonald's opposite work!

Who do you admire most and why?
Richard Branson, because he is prepared to take a risk on various business ideas, regardless of whether the company is in a sector or not. Calculated risks are a key part of an expanding business.

What is your earliest memory?
Chasing frogs around the garden.

What is the worst job you've ever done?
Tile cutting on an assembly line.

What do you consider to be your greatest achievement?
Walking the Pennine Way and then running the Great North Run within two weeks.

Have you ever won any awards or been shortlisted for anything interesting?
I was named player of the year for the Wheatsheaf Pub Sunday League in 1984.

What in your opinion will be the 'next big thing'?
Whatever it is, my nephew will want it for Christmas!

ICM Plastics is part of the Merriott Plastics Group, a well-established group of moulding companies specialising in injection and compression moulding. In fact, it's highly likely that you will have come into contact with, or will even own, a plastic component that they have produced. It could be anything from the plastic speaker guards for your stereo to the various plastic engine parts that you might have under the bonnet of your car or the junction box for your telephone.

The company employs a team of eighty people at its base on the Medway City Estate in Rochester where it has been situated for twenty-three of its impressive sixty-three years of operation. Being a large-scale producer of plastic waste, the company recognises the need for responsible waste disposal and recycles various plastics. It applies the same principles to cardboard and paper and has a full environmental policy.

As well as being environmentally aware, ICM Plastics also prides itself on delivering zero-defect work and believes its commitment to delivering work of the highest quality throughout the organisation has significantly contributed to it being a major supplier to an impressive list of customers. But the company has had to work as hard as any other in order to survive. In its early days, the company was called Insulating Components and Materials and moulded specialist materials for the Ministry of Defence and Royal Ordnance sites. Over the years it has diversified into automotive, electrical industrial fans and commercial sectors to maintain the level of business needed to continue trading.

This diversification has paid off, and ICM Plastics is now a successful business with high-profile clients in the UK, Europe and Asia, including Aston Martin, British Aerospace Defence, Marconi Defence Systems and the Ministry of Defence.

ICM Plastics
Michael Mitchelson
T: +44 (0)1634 298 512
E: Michael@icm-plasticmoulding.co.uk
W: www.merriott.com

'Our greatest achievement is exceeding our customers' expectations.'

Describe yourself in three words.
Innovative, proactive, focused.

Where are you from originally?
Japan.

Describe what you do?
Manufacturer of shrink sleeves.

Who or what inspires you?
The drive to innovate.

How long has the company been running for?
Since 1897 in Japan, and in Gillingham for twenty-one years.

Best thing about Medway?
Its close proximity to and communication links with mainland Europe.

What puts a smile on your faces?
Happy customers plus products on shelves carrying a Fuji Seal Europe shrink sleeve.

What do you consider to be your greatest achievement?
Exceeding our customers' expectations.

What is your philosophy in a nutshell?
To support our customers' growth.

Over twenty years ago Fuji Seal chose the UK for its first European plant and opted for south-east England, Medway in particular, with its convenient links to mainland Europe. Thanks to the efforts of the staff, Fuji Seal – the inventor and pioneer of shrink-sleeve technology – is a proud and flourishing manufacturer in Medway.

After starting life a little over 100 years ago in Japan, when Fuji Seal manufactured wooden plugs for sake barrels, the company progressed to the state-of-the-art packaging manufacturer it is today. In the 1960s there was a need to produce shrinkable tamper-evident cap-seals for sake bottles. At this point, Fuji Seal developed the product and introduced the first shrink sleeve for container decoration.

Fuji Seal shrink sleeves are more than just labels. Containers can be transformed to the extent that the emphasis is no longer on the container but the sleeve itself. Clients include manufacturers of some of the best-known brands on the market – Heinz, Lucozade and Surf/Persil are just a few of those that are labelled with Fuji Seal shrink sleeves – the kinds of products that sit on the shelves of supermarkets on every continent. In terms of sustainability, Fuji Seal recycles its waste film and has led the way in developing eco-friendly shrink films.

Fuji Seal Europe Ltd
T: +44 (0)1634 378656
E: sales@fujiseal.com/uk
W: www.fujiseal.com

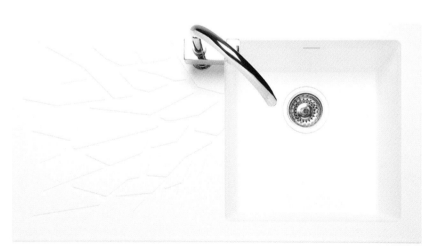

above: 'Teenyweenykins'
by Kaley Woods
E: hello@kaleywoods.co.uk
W: www. kaleywoods.co.uk

left: 'Decosink'
by Tina Hakala
E: moi@tinahakala.com
W: www.tinahakala.com

BA (Hons) Product Design
BA (Hons) Furniture Design

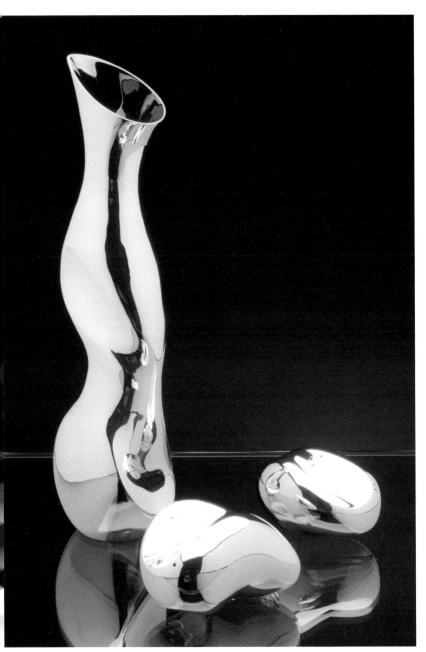

above: 'Bangle – Elegance & Refinement'
by Jennie Darbyshire
E: jendarby@hotmail.com

left: 'Ergonomic Condiments'
by Jemma Daniels
E: jemma@jemmadaniels.com
W: www.jemmadaniels.com

BA (Hons) Silversmithing, Goldsmithing and Jewellery

'A man bangs his head against a brick wall, eventually the wall falls down.'

Who or what inspires you?
Good engineering.

Best thing about Medway?
I live here.

Does your business employ any green or sustainable policies?
Yes. All waste plastic and cardboard is recycled.

What has been your most unusual commission?
Our pipe clips were used in the manufacture of pasting tables!

What puts a smile on your face?
A big order.

What is your earliest memory?
My bedroom curtains when I was about two years old.

What can't you live without?
Chocolate.

Who do you admire most and why?
The renowned engineer Isambard Kingdom Brunel.

What is the worst job you've ever done?
Assembling road-paving machines – an example of bad engineering.

What is the best piece of advice you've been given?
Try it, it might work!

What is your philosophy in a nutshell?
A man bangs his head against a brick wall, eventually the wall falls down.

Talon's founder, Mike Dudney, was selling building fixings from a tiny industrial unit in Strood when he first hit upon the idea of creating a plastic moulded pipe clip. One of his customers, a large heating and plumbing contractor, complained about the quality of pipe clips, a product that Mike didn't supply.

Having once been a toolmaker, Mike thought he would have a go at trying to make something that would both satisfy his customer's needs and ultimately enable him to sell in large quantities.

Pipe clips already existed, so he knew his design needed to be exceptional. It took him a year to perfect the design for the Talon Hinged Clip, but it was worth the wait, winning him his first order for 5,000 units. Now, twenty-two years later, Talon has sold more than 300 million and is now the market leader for pipe clips and cover profiles. It also supplies a whole range of associated fixings and fastenings plus specialist plumbing accessories to customers in the UK, Ireland and even as far afield as New Zealand.

Mike puts his success down to being a 'daydream believer' – he had a dream of running his own successful business and believed he could achieve it. From starting as a one-man band he now employs thirty-three people, and over the years Talon has won the Medway Small Business Award twice, the Kent Small Business Award twice and was runner-up in the South-East Business Awards.

It's Mike's passion for quality and great engineering that he believes has helped the business navigate through good times and bad. By creating well-designed high-quality products and recruiting a team of dedicated and professional people he believes he's set Talon in good stead to go on to achieve bigger and better things – and, as Mike has already proved, maintaining a positive attitude can drive you to achievement and success.

Talon
Mike Dudney
T: +44 (0)1634 296 960
E: sales@talon.co.uk
W: www.talon.co.uk

It's important to focus on the nuts and bolts of business.

'Don't run before you can walk – always learn the basics of your trade well before you try to move on to bigger and better things.'

Who or what inspires you?
Peter: Seeing my son evolve into a highly skilled paint-sprayer.
Wayne: My dad. He inspires me to work hard and to maintain the high standard of workmanship for which Mech-Spray is renowned.

Best thing about Medway?
Wayne: Historic Rochester for its past, and the exciting future which is evolving within the Thames Gateway.

What puts a smile on your face?
Peter: When everything goes according to plan!
Wayne: My wife's smile.

What is your earliest memory?
Peter: Going to my first motorcycle speedway meeting with my dad.
Wayne: When my dad bought me a mini motorcycle and painted it in an Evel Knievel paint scheme.

What do you consider to be your greatest achievement?
Peter: My family – we work and play together!
Wayne: Mastering the art of applying Candy Apple paintwork. Very few people can actually do this correctly.

What's the best piece of advice you've been given?
Peter: Don't run before you can walk – always learn the basics of your trade well before you try to move on to bigger and better things.

It was 1967 when top motorcyclist Paul Smart gave his friend Peter Darwell a tip-off about an auto-body shop in Medway looking for a business partner. Peter followed the lead up, but rather than just buy himself a slice of the pie he bought all the partners out and became sole proprietor of Mech-Spray.

A self-taught specialist spray-painter, Peter's previous experience was as an apprentice at a Rolls-Royce-approved body shop. He quickly earned a reputation for his work, and in 1970 he entered his first car show at Crystal Palace where he won the top award in the Best Paint category. It was a title he held for the next six consecutive years, and the first of hundreds of future awards for Mech-Spray.

A combination of Peter's raw talent and years of perfecting his technique have earned Mech-Spray its reputation as the UK's leader in custom and special-effect paintwork. While classic contours and auto work will always remain at the heart of the business, Mech-Spray also designs and applies bespoke paintwork to any surface.

For example, commissions have included painting Pink Floyd drummer Nick Mason's helicopter, the Batmobile for the film *Batman* and the Thunderbirds car. The company also works with interior-design clients such as Edward Allington and Richard Rogers, for whom Mech-Spray is the official painter and has delivered a bespoke painting for his own home.

Wayne originally studied business and finance at college. But while working for his father Peter during the holidays he was sent on a training course to learn how to use a new paint-mixing scheme. It was on this course that his natural talent was spotted – so impressive was Wayne's work that the tutor thought he was a plant from the paint company to check how well he was teaching! Wayne has now built up an impressive list of Best Paint accolades himself.

Mech-Spray is now a true family business with Wayne Darwell working alongside his father at the helm. As yet there is no third generation lined up to join the business. But Peter is a patient man; he's in no hurry to hang up his paint gun. In fact, he's only recently bought a new spray booth, which he says has years of use left in it!

Mech-Spray
Peter and Wayne Darwell
T: +44 (0)1634 847 940
E: mechspray@aol.com

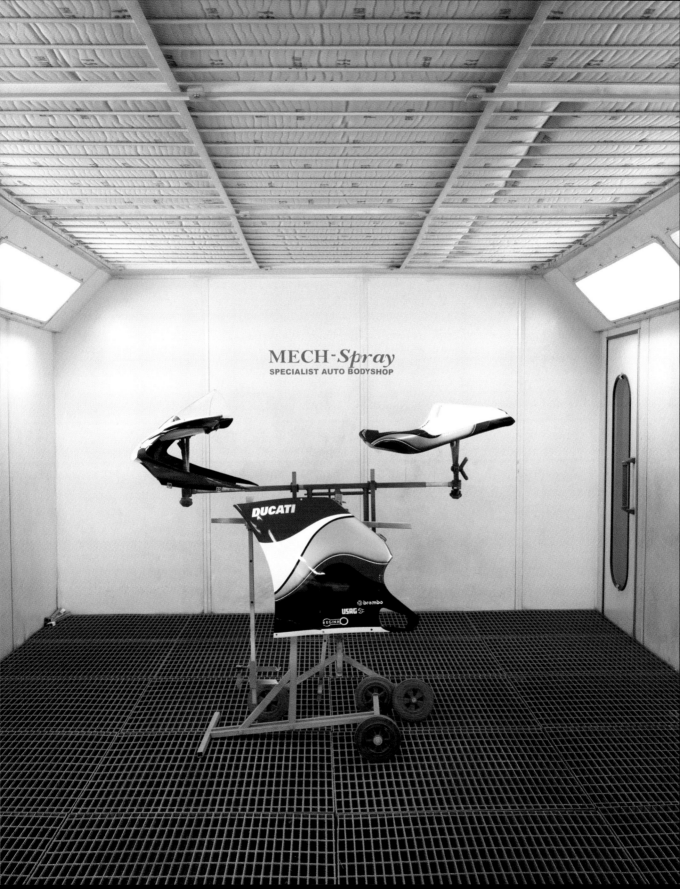

Handrail Design

'We work with many local companies and have used the same engineering company, J & A Precision Engineering, since we commenced trading.'

Describe yourself in three words.
Passionate, energetic, fun.

What has been your most unusual commission?
A viewing gallery in a mortuary!

Has the manufacturing industry changed since you've been in business?
In recent years we have seen dramatic increases in the cost of stainless steel, and so, to remain competitive, we reverse-engineered many components, enabling us to reduce the costly elements to a minimum without compromising quality and design.

What puts a smile on your face?
Opening the post in the morning and finding plenty of new orders and cheques!

Do you collaborate with any Medway companies?
We work with many local companies and have used the same engineering company, J and A Precision Engineering, since we commenced trading in 1990.

Best thing about Medway?
The Historic Dockyard.

Your greatest achievement?
Remaining sane!

What are your most overused phrases?
Harder, faster, longer!

The best piece of advice you've been given?
Don't worry, things are never as bad as they seem!

Handrail Design is based at the Sail & Colour Loft (a Grade II listed building dating back to 1734) at the Historic Dockyard in Chatham. Established in 1990 by husband-and-wife team Fiona and Howard Cochrane, who relocated from Yorkshire, Handrail Design is the most specialised modular-handrail company in the UK. It provides design, supply and installation of bespoke architectural handrail and balustrade products. Employing twenty-eight staff at their Chatham site, Handrail Design also provides business opportunities to many local businesses across the Medway area as it subcontracts out much of its work.

The business prides itself on its products being the most requested choice of UK architects. In fact, if you work in a City bank or other high-end corporate office space, then it's possible that you come into contact with Handrail Design's contemporary metal and glass products on a daily basis. As the products are for a niche market it does not undertake any domestic projects. Instead, the team prefer to work with architects on highly specialised jobs, where there is adequate space to display their products properly.

There are three main ranges: the icon CUBE®; TUBE®; and VIEU®. The icon CUBE® features uprights made from paired aluminium flats, braced together by unique CUBE® components. The icon TUBE® is the company's original tubular-based system manufactured in stainless steel, NyMet® nylon-coated aluminium or a combination of the two. The icon VIEU® offers a system solution for structural glass balustrades with stainless-steel boss fixings. While all three are patented, the designs are highly attractive, so they are often copied by lower sectors of the glass-and-metal balustrade market.

The company is also the UK's exclusive distributor of d line, a Danish-designed handrail system. Handrail Design's services are continually endorsed by leading developers, architects and contractors. So it's no surprise that the company has undertaken many landmark projects, including: the Cabinet Office; Rothschild, Regent Quarter at Kings Cross; and British Airways' corporate headquarters, for which Handrail Design received special recognition by the client for its contribution to the building's construction.

Handrail Design
Fiona and Howard Cochrane
T: +44 (0)1634 817 800
E: fiona@handraildesign.co.uk
W: www.handraildesign.co.uk

'I admire those who are happy with their lot. Satisfaction is difficult to achieve.'

Describe yourself in three words.
Small, happy, Aquarian.

Describe what you do.
I proudly present to the world natural herbal medicines and food supplements, which are made in Kent.

Who or what inspires you?
People inspire me. I'm fascinated by the life cycle and believe good transcends evil. I suppose it's called optimism!

Best thing about Medway?
It has immense character and, being so accessible to Europe, a big future.

What is your earliest memory?
I was evacuated to the Welsh countryside where I remember collecting milk in a jug from a farm that had a cow. I can still recall the taste and the smell.

Who do you admire most and why?
I admire those who are happy with their lot. Satisfaction is difficult to achieve.

In her own words, June Crisp is a 'plucky London war baby'. She started her career in haute couture with dreams of being a fashion designer, but marriage and babies changed her course, and in 1996 she bought a herbal-medicine company, Bio-Health. Originally established in 1981, Bio-Health produces additive-free vitamin, mineral and herbal supplements. It began manufacturing in Medway in 1988 and is still based at its Rochester site today.

Bio-Health's Pure-fil product range was launched the year the company was founded and featured seven additive-free supplements for the health-food market. It was quickly recognised by doctors and practitioners as a particularly helpful alternative medicine for allergy sufferers, and so the range began to take off.

As the range grew, so did the expertise within the company. When June joined the team she brought with her Victor Perfitt MBE, who immediately set about transforming the Bio-Health plant into premises that would be licensed to manufacture medicines. A full manufacturing licence was granted a year later.

The company has taken its in-house manufacturing a step further than most, planting a wild organic garden and meadow at the Rochester site. In the middle of a rather grey industrial estate is a beautiful oasis with natural plants, shrubs and trees. Not only does the garden attract birds, butterflies, bees and numerous insects but it also enables staff to see the herbs they turn into medicines in their original growing form.

As you would expect, green issues are high on Bio-Health's agenda. It has always striven to follow sustainable business practices and introduced a formal policy in 2004 that runs through every aspect of its operations, from eco-managers, who monitor utility use, to a formal waste strategy that covers paper, packaging, plastics composting and sacking and sheeting. The company has seen the waste it sends to landfill plummet from one large skip a fortnight to less than half a skip a month – and Bio-Health is committed to reducing this further still.

Bio-Health's commitment to green issues, along with its overall business success, has seen it collect a number of awards. As well as Victor's MBE, the first ever to be awarded for work in herbal medicine, the company was also named 2004 Fastest Achieving Small Business and was a finalist in the SEEDA Sustainable Business Awards 2006.

June has boundless enthusiasm for Bio-Health and says owning a manufacturing company she is immensely proud of is her greatest achievement.

Bio-Health
June Crisp
T: +44 (0)1634 290 115
E: info@bio-health.co.uk
W: www.bio-health.co.uk

"Thinking is the most fundamental and important human skill!"
Edward De Bono

Saxon Engineering

'The necessity to multitask is essential – now more than ever.'

Describe yourself in three words.
Amenable, dependable, honest.

Describe what you do.
Machine components in any material, anytime, for anybody!

Who or what inspires you?
Success and successful people.

Best thing about Medway?
The location.

What materials do you specialise in?
Non-ferrous – 6082 aluminium.

What has been your most unusual commission?
Figure moulded in a Perspex ball – machined spherical.

What is your earliest memory?
Saying goodbye to a school friend who was leaving London.

What is the best piece of advice you've been given?
Don't burn any bridges.

Has the manufacturing industry changed since you've been in business?
Yes. The necessity to multitask is essential – now more than ever.

Your most overused phrases?
Better day tomorrow.

Your philosophy in a nutshell?
Do the right thing.

In 1989 Steve Parker Smith decided to sell his motorcycle, buy a lathe with the proceeds and set up his own company. His father-in-law found him a small milling machine and, after some inevitable banging on doors, he soon had the machines humming away producing work. Saxon Engineering was now in business.

Based in Gillingham, the company produces high-standard precision metalwork and over the past nineteen years has grown at a steady rate. This growth has been aided by Steve's significant investment in the business, providing the latest engineering technology to maintain the company's high quality and competitive edge.

The company uses Computer Aided Design (CAD) and Computer Aided Manufacture (CAM). Its highly skilled team of nine can tackle anything, from a one-off copy of an existing part through to a large quantity of complex CAD components. It has DNC links to its CNC milling machines and also has impressive turning capabilities – both CNC and manual. To ensure absolute precision, Saxon Engineering also has a co-ordinate measuring machine (CMM) and the very latest in gauging technology so customers can be assured of the accuracy of its work – down to three-thousandths of a millimetre to be precise!

Among the many diverse products the company manufactures are prototype car-engine parts, medical equipment, military-barrel systems and newsprint and press equipment. It has an impressive customer base, including Fuji Seal, Dana, Proctor and Gamble and Thales. Steve and his team are passionate about what they do, and armed with their commitment to providing the most technologically advanced precision engineering they firmly believe they will attract further top-flight customers in the future. It's amazing what you can achieve with the price of a motorbike!

Saxon Engineering
Steve Parker Smith
T: +44 (0)1634 370 023
E: saxoneng@aol.com
W: www.saxonengineering.com

M.C. Air Filtration

'There are always more questions than answers.'

Describe yourself in three words.
Grumpy old man.

Who or what inspires you?
The poem 'If' by Rudyard Kipling.

Best thing about Medway?
Its proximity to motorways, the high-speed rail link, the Weald of Kent and the seaside.

What puts a smile on your face?
Only Fools and Horses.

What is your earliest memory?
My first day at school.

What can't you live without?
A pint of bitter.

Who do you admire most and why?
Sir David Attenborough, a most remarkable human being and pioneer of natural-history presentation.

Your most overused phrase?
There are always more questions than answers.

If you're looking for a breath or two of fresh, not to mention totally clean, air then you should head to Gillingham-based M.C. Air Filtration. The company, established in 1974, is one of Britain's leading designers and manufacturers of precision particulate and gaseous filtration systems.

Over the years the company has developed an extensive portfolio of products and services for diverse markets such as the microelectronic, pharmaceutical, research, health, decontamination, defence and nuclear industries. Not surprising then that you can find its air filters in any number of unusual places. From armoured fighting vehicles to warships, nuclear power stations, hospitals, laboratories and factories. In fact, they've even provided environmental protection to the Crown Jewels in the Tower of London!

It's not just clean that M.C. Air Filtration does well, it's green too. All forty-five staff at the company are committed to improving the environment, and, as General Manager Gary John describes, they 'recycle with a vengeance'. As the company works primarily in metals, glass and plastics, it's good to see it takes its environmental responsibilities seriously.

The company also recognises the importance of consistent quality assurance and has manufactured products to ISO 9001 since 1991. It also currently holds ISO 9001:2000 for design and manufacture of high-efficiency air filters, nuclear and biological air filters with associated housings, portable air-filtration units for contaminated areas and clean-room filter installations.

With thirty-four years of manufacturing under its belt, M.C. Air Filtration has seen the sector change dramatically. To stay one step ahead it has taken the deliberate measure of developing into niche product areas, working with customers to create bespoke products to meet their specific requirements. It's this tailored approach that the company believes will set it in good stead for the future.

M.C. Air Filtration
Gary John
T: +44 (0)1634 388 333
E: garyjohn@mcaf.co.uk
W: www.mcaf.co.uk

MC Modelmaking

'I like the history around every corner: the 19th-century stuff, the dockyard, the old theatres and the individual stories of Medway characters.'

Describe yourself in three words.
Obsessed with detail.

Who or what inspires you?
I've always been inspired by films and am often out videoing junk and old buildings. Modelmakers are an odd bunch, we get excited about fast-acting glues and interesting bits of plastic! I get obsessed with buildings – last year was my George Gilbert Scott phase.

Who do you admire most?
My wife Julia for putting up with me and my precious collections of … stuff!

Your most unusual commission?
A recreation of the Jezreel's Tower, Gillingham. The Jezreelites (a religious sect who never cut their hair) started building it but never finished. This job involved extensive research, as the full set of original drawings has never been found.

Best things about Medway?
I like the rough with the smooth and the history around every corner: the 19th-century stuff, the dockyard, the old theatres and the individual stories of Medway characters. Just a couple of months ago I discovered we have one of Shaftsbury's Ragged Schools in Chatham.

What is the worst job you've ever done?
Sorting laundry at the old Oakwood Park Psychiatric Hospital. Dirty laundry …

Your most overused phrases?
At work, 'how much?'; at home, 'Get over it!'

Your greatest achievement?
Getting up this morning …

As a child Martin Earle was spellbound by the antics of Jason and the Argonauts (fighting skeletons) and King Kong (wrestling dinosaurs). This fascination led to him spending hours in his parents' loft animating Plasticine models – which, in turn, was the catalyst for studying Interior Design at the University for the Creative Arts and modelmaking at Hertfordshire University.

After working for various architects and modelmakers in London, Martin grew sick of commuting, took the plunge, and in 1994 he set up MC Modelmaking. He borrowed a garden workshop for a year, then rented a room above the stables in the dockyard. Business took off, and in 2002 they moved to their current premises also in the dockyard.

MC Modelmaking has over fourteen years' experience of manufacturing in Medway, specialising in producing architectural and industrial models for advertising, architects, developers, display and exhibitions. Museum and diagrammatic models are also a specialism – the resin dinosaurs and skeletons are eerily lifelike! Working closely with architects, designers, engineers and landscape architects, the company's team of modelmakers work with CAD drawings to produce accurate architectural detailing. In terms of materials, they use metal, wood, plastics (acrylic and high-density polystyrene), silicon and PU resins teamed with an extensive knowledge of CAD, fibre-optic lighting, laser cutting and engraving. Furthermore, the company is actively reducing its carbon footprint by recycling and re-processing 40–50 per cent of its waste materials.

As with most industries, email and the internet has changed the way the company works. Communication has leapt forward at an incredible pace and presented whole new ways of doing things. A decade ago, the first time a client saw their model was on the day of delivery. Today, artwork is drawn and adjusted by CAD, and progress shots are emailed to the client on a regular basis.

MC Modelmaking's clients include Dickens World, Countryside Properties, the Houses of Parliament Education Service, SEEDA, the Tower of London and Thames Water. Architectural models are frequently shipped overseas to the USA, Europe and Hong Kong.

MC Modelmaking Ltd
Martin Earle
T: +44(0)1634 818 539
E: enquiries@mcmodelmaking.co.uk
W: www.mcmodelmaking.co.uk

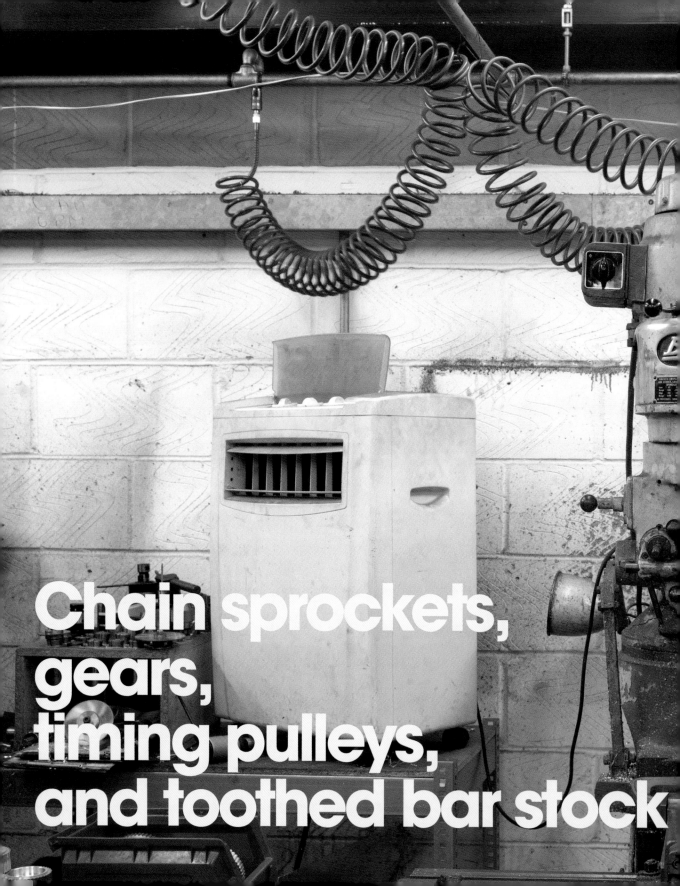

Chain sprockets, gears, timing pulleys, and toothed bar stock

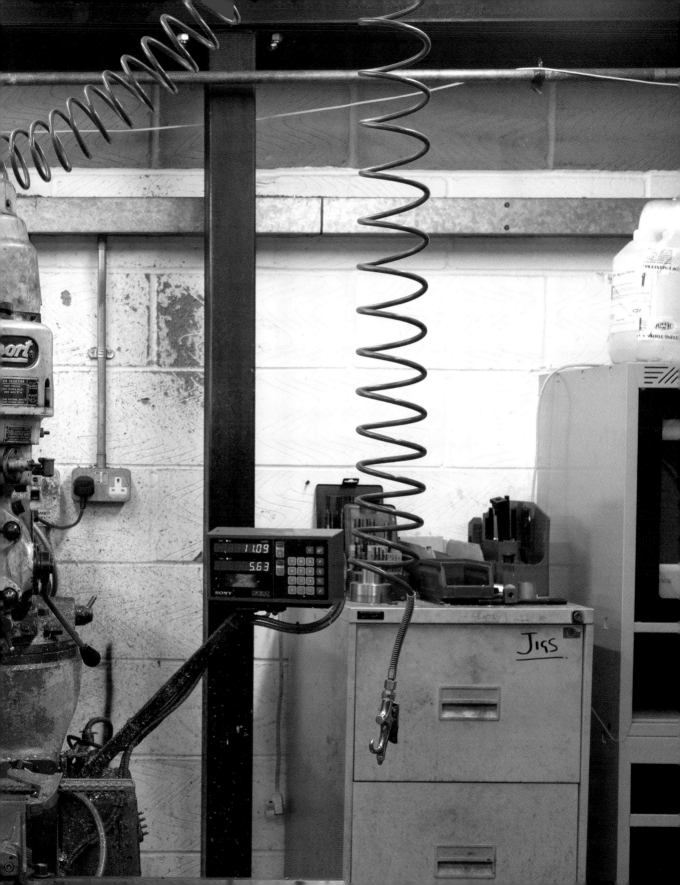

Hydraulic and Engineering Services

'Medway is part of the busiest environment in the south yet close enough to Kent to get away from it all for some rest and relaxation.'

Describe yourself in three words.
Fair, driven, realistic.

Who or what inspires you?
Life! You just have to get on with it because it can be taken in the blink of an eye.

Best thing about Medway?
Medway is part of the busiest environment in the south yet close enough to Kent to get away from it all for some rest and relaxation.

What puts a smile on your face?
My two sons, the sunshine, winning a good order and seeing work go out of the door that one can be proud of.

Your earliest memory?
As a small boy I lived in flats by the *Cutty Sark* in Greenwich. One of my earliest memories is opening the front door to find the Thames had flooded. The water was lapping at the doorstep and in front of me was what looked like a big lake.

What is the worst job you've ever done?
As a schoolboy I cleaned a mincing machine in a shop – too many wriggly things for my liking!

Who do you admire most and why?
I admire entrepreneurs like Richard Branson. They know how to motivate people to get the best from them and can reward them well.

Your philosophy in a nutshell?
Life is precious and precarious, enjoy today but put a few nuts away for tomorrow as you never know what is around the corner.

A toolmaker by trade, Stephen Matthews, who hails from Greenwich originally, went into the hydraulics business when he was twenty-four. Three years later he set up his own company, Hydraulic and Engineering Services Ltd, and hasn't looked back since. That was eighteen years ago, and he now employs a team of just under forty at the company's large manufacturing and repair facility on the Medway City Estate in Strood.

Hydraulic and Engineering Services Ltd operates a versatile service, committed to the manufacture, supply and repair of high-quality hydraulic cylinders, repairs and equipment to the crane, industrial, mobile-plant and marine markets. Working mainly with high-grade steels, the company has an impressive capacity to handle cylinders of up to 10 metres in length, 0.8 metres in diameter and in excess of 4 tonnes in weight. Stephen admits that engineering is not an easy business, especially in his field of service and specialist manufacture. But he thrives on the challenge that change brings and so is constantly working with his team to adapt and innovate. It's the company's commitment to innovation that wins it high-profile and sometimes unusual projects. One of the most memorable to date has been delivering the hydraulics for the West End show *We Will Rock You*, and later its spin-off travelling show.

Quality is also an important driver for Stephen. As well as being a member of the British Fluid Power Distributors Association, he operates the business to ISO 9000:2000 and believes this has been an important factor in helping him win a number of grants that have helped him grow the business.

Looking to the future, Stephen has plans to continue expanding the company. He maintains that as the projects coming through the door become ever larger and more technical, so too will Hydraulic and Engineering Services – music to Stephen's ears!

Hydraulic and Engineering Services Ltd
Stephen Matthews
T: +44 (0)1634 295 650
E: steve@hydraulicandengineering.co.uk
W: www.hydraulicandengineering.co.uk

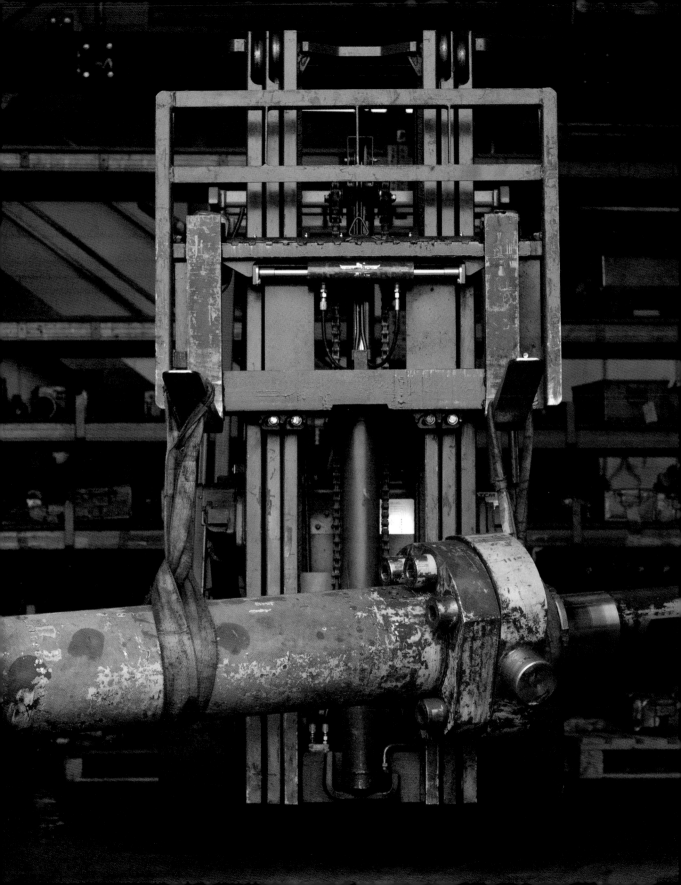

'Gillingham FC is the best and worst thing about Medway!'

Describe yourself in three words.
Direct, confident, loyal.

What is your earliest memory?
My camping holidays in Hastings. Things were tight in those days, and we borrowed an army bell tent. It was double the size of anything on the campsite and it leaked. We looked out of place and felt a bit soggy, but I still loved it.

Who or what inspires you?
Life inspires me; sport, history and great things done by ordinary people.

Who do you admire most and why?
My man's man is Simon Weston. A true hero, he managed to make good from a bad situation.

What are your most overused phrases?
I need it ASAP!

What in your opinion will be the 'next big thing'?
I'm going to talk to Richard Branson about a countrywide chain of mobility outlets – perhaps we'll call it Virgin Mobility? It's the only thing left that he hasn't done on a nationwide scale. Richard is unaware of my plan, but if anyone speaks to him first then I will sue!

Your philosophy in a nutshell?
Life is about choices, chances and the problems put in front of us. I believe most of us can influence the path we take, so my philosophy is if things aren't going the way you want, don't moan, just try to change them.

Wayne Cotter, a Gillingham man born and bred, has always worked with his hands. He initially wanted to become a carpenter, but after landing a job working as a chippy he quickly reconsidered. Deciding that carpentry wasn't for him, Wayne changed career, joining Rehabilitation Manufacturing Services (RMS) instead.

Gillingham-based RMS is one of the UK's most respected manufacturers and suppliers of customised wheelchairs and disablement accessories. As Wayne worked his way through the ranks at RMS he held steadfast to his mantra that whenever a challenge was put in front of him, he would take it on. So when the opportunity to undertake an MBO presented itself, he and colleagues Del Bryant and Alan Wombell decided to go for it. The decision has paid off, and Wayne and his fellow company directors now run a successful team of thirty-six people.

Most of RMS's work comes from the NHS, but this is gradually beginning to diversify as it has started to sell to other companies to export. While working with the NHS brings in lucrative work for the company, it has had to adapt its manufacturing processes in order to keep up with demand, reducing production times from weeks to days.

Because of the nature of its business, the company works with all sorts of materials, from wood, metal and plastics to laminate and foam. Its most popular product is the Gillingham Tilt wheelchair and accessories. RMS makes customised wheelchairs for children too, manufacturing them in funky, vibrant colours. It's a sensitive market but the company's experience enables it to understand and respond to its young customers' needs.

One of the most unusual challenges the company has faced was making a seat for a local girl with a hyper-sensitive coccyx. The RMS team came up with a design that left the area around the pressure point void, thus avoiding contact. It's projects like this, where they help relieve pain and give people their independence back, that give Wayne and the RMS team their greatest satisfaction.

Rehabilitation Manufacturing Services
Wayne Cotter
T: +44 (0)1634 578 881
E: sales@rms-kent.co.uk
W: www.ineedawheelchair.co.uk

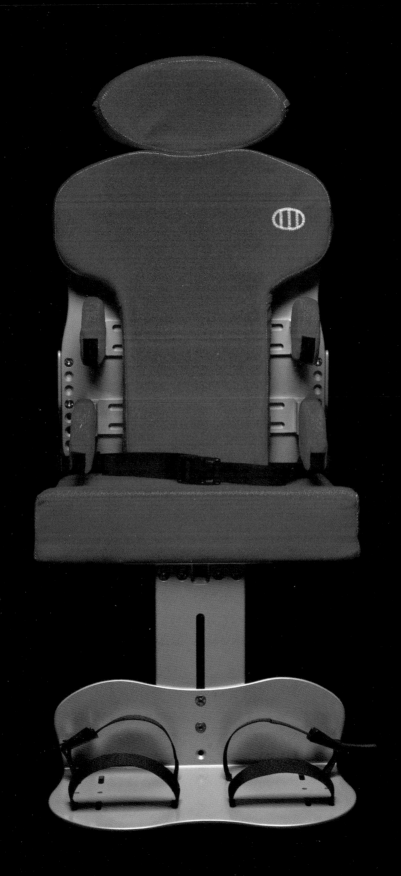

'You will always find time for something you really want to do.'

Describe yourself in three words
Reliable, thorough, trustworthy.

Best thing about Medway?
The view of the River Medway from our workrooms and the access we have to the countryside.

Who or what inspires you?
My wife and family and Beethoven.

What do you consider to be your greatest achievement?
Still being in business after thirty-five years.

What has been your most unusual commission?
Opening-ceremony curtains made from the Stars and Stripes and the Union Jack flags for the opening of the first McDonald's restaurant in the UK.

What puts a smile on your face?
Our employees having a laugh and a joke and enjoying their work.

What is your earliest memory?
Being cradled in my mother's arms as we hid behind a wardrobe during a V-2 raid on London – I was only two.

What can't you live without?
My wife, golf and Arsenal.

What is the best piece of advice you've been given?
You will always find time for something you really want to do.

What is your philosophy in a nutshell?
Do the best job for the client but enjoy life at the same time.

When Mick Porter was training to become an aeronautical engineer, it's doubtful he imagined he would go on to have a long and successful career in soft furnishings. But that's exactly what he has achieved. The working-class lad from north London set up Deanswood Interiors with his wife, herself a trained curtain-maker, back in 1983.

Thirty-five years later, and Deanswood Interiors is one of the leading suppliers of high-quality curtains, blinds, soft furnishings and upholstery to architects and interior designers. The company still uses traditional skills, and so the level of craftsmanship is second to none. It's therefore not surprising to learn that Deanswood Interiors has furnished some prestigious residences, including the Lord Mayor of London's official apartment and Edward Heath's Salisbury residence.

Deanswood's industrial-sized workroom is based in Rochester and has views across the River Medway. It needs to be large to accommodate the huge drops of the curtains the company makes. A team of sixteen curtain-makers, project managers, fitters and support staff work together at the site to produce breathtaking curtains and furnishings.

While most of the company's clients are London based, the projects they work on are both national and international, and so Deanswood's work can be found anywhere from the Cayman Islands to Canada to France.

As Mick looks to the future he stands firm that there will always remain a strong market for traditional high-quality soft furnishings. But he has also identified the growth in the use of intelligent technology in interior design. Capitalising on this opportunity, Deanswood Interiors has joined forces with Adapt Control Systems and Total Media to offer its clients home-automation solutions, whereby systems such as heating, lighting, entertainment and even curtains, can be controlled by one central device. Perhaps the engineer in him is still alive and kicking after all?

Deanswood
Mick Porter
T: +44 (0)1634 814444
E: mickp@deanswood.co.uk
W: www.deanswood.co.uk

Pioneering research fuelled by a background of medical physics, electronics and bioengineering.

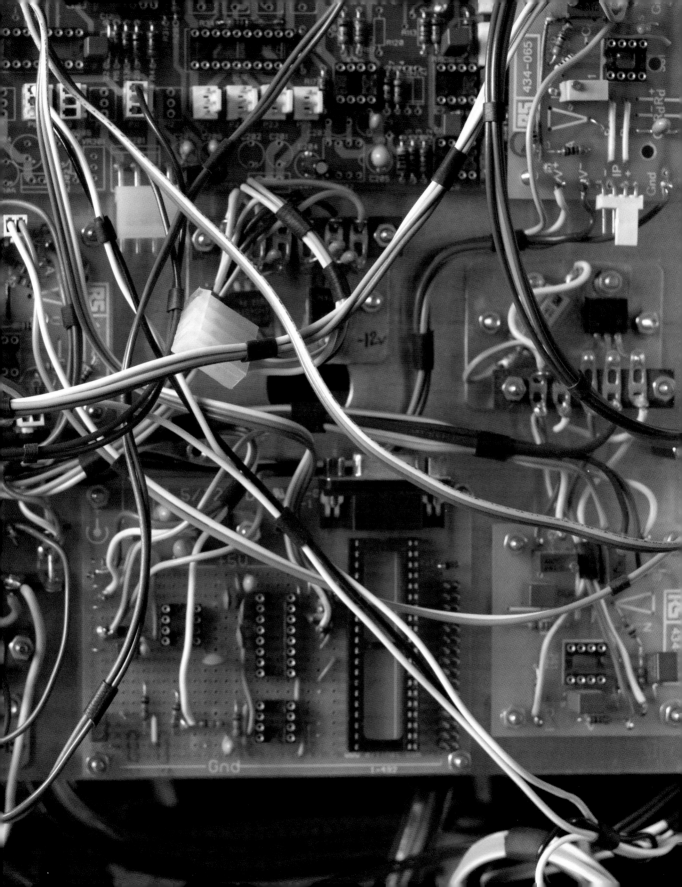

Kelly Norman Engineering

'Times change, values don't.'

Describe yourself in three words.
Determined, optimistic, getting on!

What is the best piece of advice you've been given?
Times change, values don't.

What inspires you?
Need, greed and interest.

What puts a smile on your face?
A smile on someone else's face!

What is your earliest memory?
Tying my first shoelace.

What has been your most unusual commission?
A difficult choice. Millbank Pier probably.

What can't you live without?
Potatoes.

What do you consider to be your greatest achievement?
The QE2 Pier at the O2.

What are your most overused phrases?
Send me an email.

What is your philosophy in a nutshell?
Time is short; do it now.

If you've always fancied living or working by the river but can't afford a riverside property then you need to speak to Kelly Norman. The Rainham-based company specialises in floating accommodation and will design a home or office that meets your exact requirements. But if you're in the marine sector, that's not all they can do …

When K&N Welding first began trading in 1983 it provided high-quality welding services for the UK civil and marine construction industry. In 1985 the business moved to Medway, and as it grew it moved into steel fabrication, handing projects ranging from single up to 300-tonne structures. With over twenty years' manufacturing experience in Medway, the company has built up a loyal client base.

Since the late 1990s Kelly Norman has concentrated on the marine sector and manufactures marine products ranging from commercial public piers and access brows to crane and flat-top barges, floating homes and offices. In addition, it offers a service providing shock-absorbing pile guides and pontoon linking systems. In 2003 Kelly Norman MAV was formed with the sole purpose of developing further marine projects.

Today the company has an impressive portfolio of high-profile projects under its belt. As well as working on the award-winning Millbank Pier outside the Tate, the Queen Elizabeth Pier at the O2 and on various pontoons for the RNLI, it recently designed and built City Cruises plc's new head office at Cherry Garden Pier on the Thames. The pontoon was built to replace the existing pontoon and Portakabin that staff were working from. The pontoon's final weight was 115 tonnes with ballast and featured an innovative macerating sewage treatment system, air conditioning, telecommunications and its own power supply.

Co-founder Kevin Kelly is justifiably proud of the high-quality work the twelve-strong Kelly Norman team delivers for its clients, naming the QE2 Pier as his personal greatest achievement. As he looks to the future he maintains his ongoing belief that change is essential in what will hold the company in good stead.

Kelly Norman
Kevin Kelly
T: +44 (0)1634 232 244
E: knwelding@btconnect.com
W: www.kellynorman.com

The Food Machinery Company

'Medway has a good support structure for small companies.'

Describe yourself in three words.
Sales, service, quality.

What inspires you?
Engineering and yacht racing.

What has been your most unusual commission?
Designing a display system for showing fruit processing for the Body Shop.

What puts a smile on your face?
A satisfied client.

Best thing about Medway?
Medway has a good support structure for small companies.

What is the worst job you've ever done?
Fitting a three-metre by two-metre extraction canopy to an eight-metre-high ceiling overnight!

Your most overused phrase?
Can you just ...

Your philosophy in a nutshell?
Treat staff and customers the same way that you would wish to be treated yourself.

It was 1979 when Mike Wilkinson decided he wanted to become his own boss. At the time he was working for a food-machinery company, but he knew he could do better, and that's when The Food Machinery Company was born. It was originally based in Erith but relocated fifteen years ago. At the time Mike was looking for somewhere that was good value, had great transport links and the space they needed to expand. He came across a character property in Rochester, and the company has been there ever since.

The Food Machinery Company manufactures and supplies food-processing and packaging machinery to the catering trade. From large-scale catering ovens to food coolers, meat processors, bakery hygiene equipment and samosa makers, where kitchen, packing and cooking equipment is concerned, they pretty much have it covered.

The company employs a team of twelve at its Rochester-based factory, which features a full development kitchen for demonstrations and product development as well as a fully equipped machine shop for the manufacture of bespoke equipment. Clients range from small and medium-sized companies to large international corporations, situated in the UK, Ireland and the Middle East. Its biggest order to date has been a £3 million five-year contract with McDonald's Restaurants – a far cry from the company's first order back in 1979 of just £30!

It is large-scale orders such as the McDonald's contract that have enabled Mike to grow the business. He is currently in the process of expanding his premises to install a larger kitchen showroom, and he's determined to earn a carbon stamp for the project so it will be a carefully considered eco-friendly, energy-efficient renovation.

Since moving to the Medway area, The Food Machine Company has gone from strength to strength, and its success has been recognised in the Kent Business Growth Awards, which the company won in 2001 and was runner-up in 1999 and 2003. Mike's buzzword for future success is 'organic'. Along with SMEs, it's his fastest-growing client sector, and he predicts that the more we demand organic food, the more organic food companies will demand his products!

The Food Machinery Company
Mike Wilkinson
T: +44 (0)1634 272 345
E: sales@foodmc.com
W: www.foodmc.com

'The help you can get from Business Link and the Chamber of Commerce have been invaluable to us.'

Describe yourself in three words.
Determined, hardworking, ambitious.

Who or what inspires you?
Our customers and my workforce – wherever possible we work as a team. The results have been amazing and hopefully will continue to be so.

What puts a smile on your face?
A nice big order!

Best thing about Medway?
The help you can get from Business Link and the Chamber of Commerce have been invaluable to us. Medway also has superb travel links.

Who do you admire most?
Richard Branson, he did everything from nothing and still takes on a challenge.

Your most overused phrase?
The customer is always right, even when he's wrong.

What do you consider to be your greatest achievement?
Breaking the £1 million turnover mark.

What is the best piece of advice you've ever received?
If you don't try you won't know if you can do it.

Classic filters is, as the name suggests, a class act. The company manufactures industrial filters, which are mainly used in petrochemical gas analysis. These are extremely high-efficiency filters that can end up anywhere from spacecraft to oil refineries to the test beds for Formula 1 cars.

Based in Medway City Estate, the company was started in July 2001 by Ian Bovington, who hails originally from Gravesend. He trained as an apprentice draughtsman for a large refrigeration and air-conditioning business in Dartford, then moved to a filter company twenty-two years ago as a design engineer. He then helped establish another filter company, Headline Filters Ltd, where he was Engineering Director, before setting up Classic Filters, which now employs ten people.

The two sides of the company are: (a) replacement filter elements (manufactured from borosilicate glass microfibres) and (b) the filter housings that these elements fit into (mainly constructed from 316L SS). Classic Filters has the widest range of filter housings available for the instrumentation market, suitable for both gas and liquid applications, with ports from 3.17 to 50.8 millimetres NPT and pressures from 7 to 700 bar. All housings have CE marks if required. As well as stainless steel, housings can be supplied in a wide range of such exotic materials as Hastelloy, Monel, titanium and plastics, including PTFE, PVDF, PP and PA.

Because the filtration industry is becoming more quality orientated, companies are now ordering with short lead times. As a result, Classic Filters has had to adapt to an increasingly demanding market. Manufacturing methods have had to be changed to give the capacity to produce specialist filters at short notice. While this was costly and difficult at the time, it has now paid dividends. Export accounts for 98 per cent of the business, the company selling mostly through distributors worldwide to clients from South America to Singapore.

Classic Filters was shortlisted for the Medway Small Business Awards in 2004 and was runner-up in 2005. BP and Ferrari Formula 1 are two of the high-profile clients who use the company's products.

Classic Filters
Ian Bovington
T: +44 (0)1634 724 224
E: ian@classicfilters.com
W: www.classicfilters.com

Exotic woods such as bubinga, strawberry and ebony, certified by the Forestry Stewardship Council.

ELM BURR

Aeropsace Tooling

'Medway is in an excellent location with good road networks.'

Describe yourself in three words.
Honest, hardworking and reliable.

Best thing about Medway?
It is in an excellent location for road networks.

The best piece of advice you've been given?
Think twice …

What do you consider to be your greatest achievement?
My sons.

What can't you live without?
Chocolate.

Has the manufacturing industry changed since you've been in business?
Yes, it's now much more competitive and there are faster turnaround times for everything.

Managing Director John Seaton established Aerospace Tooling in January 2007. It is one of the largest privately owned companies of this type in the UK today, providing precision-manufacturing services to the aerospace industry and other cutting-edge suppliers along with bespoke tooling, gauges, special-purpose machine tools and lifting equipment to name but a few of their products. Although a relatively new company, it has expanded rapidly and now employs ninety people at three manufacturing locations across the UK, with Gillingham the company's head office and main base.

A wide range of materials is used, mainly metals including chrome, steel and aluminium. Essentially a precision-engineering company, it specialises in tooling and gauging and can manufacture bespoke equipment to clients' exacting specifications. For example, when it comes to cutter grinding, drills ranging from 0.5 millimetres to 60 millimetres in diameter (any angle or form) can be reground or re-formed.

To meet these requirements, Aerospace Tooling adheres to routinely audited ISO 9001 procedures, with the quality of manufacturing being underwritten by their internal calibration laboratory. Customers can also benefit from the rigid testing facilities, which include pressure testing, calibration and cutter grinding. Aerospace Tooling also offers a design service that includes simulation, CAD (Unigraphics and AutoCAD), data transfer and project management.

Aerospace Tooling boasts an impressive range of clients mainly within the aerospace and automotive industries, and it is among the leading manufacturers in its business sector. Clients include British Energy, BAE Systems, the Ministry of Defence, Ford, JCB, Land Rover and Rolls-Royce. The UK (where its customers are based) is a strong market for the company.

Aerospace Tooling Ltd
Kevan Day
T: +44(0)1634 233 216
E: k.day@aerospace-tooling.co.uk
W: www.aerospace-tooling.co.uk

Arcola Products

'There is a growing ability here to take on new challenges. After the dockyard closed many predicted doom and gloom, but Medway now has plenty of thriving industries.'

Describe yourself in three words.
Innovative, energetic, demanding.

Best thing about Medway?
There is a growing ability here to take on new challenges. After the dockyard closed many predicted doom and gloom, but Medway now has plenty of thriving industries.

Does your business employ any green or sustainable policies?
Being in the plastics industry it's not easy, but we now recycle 95 per cent of our waste. We have made arrangements to sell our scrap and look for projects that can reuse the material waste that we produce.

Your most unusual commission?
Producing female bodices from a tool supplied to us by a Rochester customer. The tool was a replica of his girlfriend and the profile opened a few eyes!

Who do you admire most?
Margaret Thatcher (cliché though it is). She came to power in difficult times and to me her steely determination always shone though.

Your greatest achievement?
Keeping the business going during really hard times of manufacturing, when we are under constant pressure from the Far East to keep our costs down.

What in your opinion will be the 'next big thing'?
Non-oil-based plastics!

First and foremost, Arcola Products is a family business based in Rainham. It was established in 1966 by Gerald Bowra, who was a pattern-maker in the engineering industry. Having recently retired, he handed over the company reins to son Dean in 2007. Born and bred in Medway, Dean worked for his father in the school holidays, completed his A-levels, then cut his teeth as a claims handler in a large insurance company. 'It gave me good experience in dealing with the public, as I started two weeks after the 1987 hurricane,' he says.

The company is primarily a vacuum former, using ABS, HIPS, polypropylene, polycarbonate and PETG, with the remainder of their work growing in the world of acrylic (Perspex and Plexiglas®) fabrication. The majority of its vacuum-formed products are bespoke products and tools, manufactured to their clients' exacting specifications.

In addition to this, Arcola also undertake pattern- and mould-making in wood and resin as well as fabrication, hinging/solvent welding and the printing of vinyl graphics. It offers an in-house design service and operates an advice line for product designers.

With over forty years' solid experience of manufacturing in Medway, customers can be assured of a comprehensive and professional service. The company employs nine members of staff, who have expertise in design, production, pattern-making, heat-forming and finishing. Unusually for a plastics company, they have managed to consistently recycle 95 per cent of their waste material. As with most manufacturing industries, Arcola has seen a change in industry pace resulting from new technologies. Consequently, it has invested in new equipment to expand its manufacturing processes because there is a continual change in clients' demands according to what styles are 'in or out'.

Arcola operates within a diverse market, including aircraft, computer companies, the education sector, food manufacturers and the medical, military and retail fields. Another string to the company's bow is fabricating acrylic products for display and point of sale, with clients including Boots and Marks & Spencer. In terms of customer geography, the UK is a strong market, as is Belfast, Dublin and the USA.

Arcola Products Ltd
Dean Bowra
T: +44(0)1634 360 562
E: info@arcolaproducts.co.uk
W: www.arcolaproducts.co.uk

Expert skills and knowledge ensures the Faraday Test Centre is a market leader in product development and qualification.

APG Developments

'Medway is in an ideal locality for good employees.'

Describe yourself in three words.
Ambitious, careful, thoughtful.

Where are you from originally?
Always from Medway.

Best thing about Medway?
Its ideal locality for good employees.

Your most unusual commission?
A 1922 aircraft propeller pulley.

Your earliest memory?
Monkeys in Gibraltar!

Who do you admire most?
My mother and sister, for their strength in life.

The best piece of advice you've been given?
If you have nothing nice to say, say nothing.

What do you consider to be your greatest achievement?
APG Developments.

Your most overused phrase?
I will call you back!

Your philosophy in a nutshell?
Work hard and play hard.

APG (which stands for All Pulley and Gear Developments) has been running since 1988 and manufacturing in Medway for twenty years. Managing Director Colin Florey saw the potential for creating the company after previously working for Medway Power Transmissions, which could not compete in today's climate and has now gone bust.

Starting from humble beginnings in a run-down back-street garage in Gillingham, APG has since gone from strength to strength. They now employ thirteen people and operate from a substantially larger 830-square-metre production base in Medway's City Estate business park. Describing itself as 'one of the leading manufacturers of special transmission products in the UK', APG has effectively found a niche market as specialist manufacturers of STD and special timing-belt drives, timing and vee-pulleys and gears and sprockets in aluminium, brass, stainless steel and plastics.

Their remit is far and wide; it's not so much a case of what they can do than what they can't do! APG can produce parts for a whole host of market sectors – cars, aeroplanes, helicopters, bomb-disposal vehicles, cash dispensers, packaging machines, boats, submarines and tractors, not to mention remote-controlled vehicles.

Utilising the latest in CNC technology it offers a range of machining facilities, including CNC turning, gear hobbing, gear shaping, metric and classical tooth forms as well as producing bespoke timing pulleys to the exact specifications of customer drawings. Extra facilities available on request to clients include gear cutting, broaching, anodising and chemical blacking.

It has an impressive client base, both in the UK and USA, which includes the Ministry of Defence, Motorola, the Post Office, Ricardo and Sunseeker luxury yachts.

APG Developments
Colin Florey
T: +44 (0)1634 722 420
E: cdf@apgdev.co.uk
W: www.apgdev.com

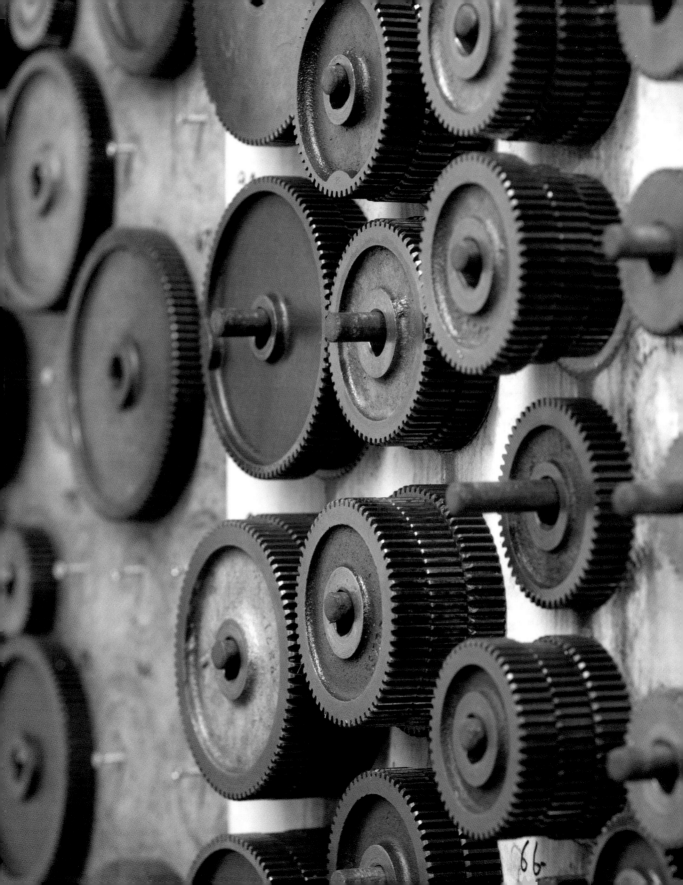

Fountain Workshop

'Our staff are our biggest asset and we're really proud of the team than we've created around us.'

What has been your most unusual commission?
David: It has to be the highest gravity-fed fountain in the world at Stanway House near Cheltenham for Lord Neidpath. Creating a 300-foot-high fountain with no pumps is certainly one of the most challenging engineering tasks we've ever undertaken, but it's one of the achievements that I'm most proud of over the years.

Best thing about Medway?
David: DIversity and a sense of constant adaptation and change, in a positive sense!
Ian: It's proved to be a wonderful location for us, and our clients always relish the opportunity to visit.

Who or what inspires you?
Ian: Working in an industry like ours it's impossible not to be inspired by the past. There is a long tradition of water in the built environment, and we're fortunate to be able to add to that story. What embraces and unites us is the inspiration that we draw from this exciting and hugely versatile medium and a sense that our work can really enhance both individual and collective well being.

Your philosophy in a nutshell?
Ian: Our staff are our biggest asset and we're really proud of the team than we've created around us. Collectively our shared vision and drive is one of our key strengths.
David: I'm proud of our diligence and the fact that we don't cut corners, despite the fact that it's probably cost us money over the years. I think the bigger picture is in the long-term benefit of that approach.

When Ian Kirkpatrick met David Bracey in 1986 they shared a common fascination – the creation of water fountains as an form. After working together at two other fountain companies, they set up The Fountain Workshop Ltd in 1996, primarily to fulfil their joint ambition of creating an innovative design-led business specialising in fountains, water features and water-related artworks. Managing Director Ian went to art college initially, later diversifying into fountains in 1980 after a stint as an architectural modelmaker. Technical Director David started out as a design draughtsman before his fortuitous meeting with Ian.

The company has always been based in Medway, initially at the Hopewell Drive Centre and then more recently at the Lead and Paint Mill, the Historic Dockyard, Chatham. Medway was chosen as a base because of its large-scale engineering network, a vital requirement for a business such as The Fountain Workshop.

But if you are looking for examples of its work then you'll have to bypass the English country gardens of Kent and head further afield. The fountains designed and produced by Ian and David's company are major pieces of high-level sculpture with a real 'wow' factor – think amazing volcanic-style fog and erupting geysers and you'll get the picture.

From the More London Development to the O2 Arena and V&A, their high-profile water features are designed to attract maximum attention. Because of the diverse range of clients and environments, The Fountain Workshop team make use of a wide range of materials. One week they can be working with a historic bronze casting or carved marble bowl and the next a new sculptural piece in stainless steel. However, the one constant is water!

So impressive is the company's reputation that, even without advertising, it has back-to-back commissions for the next two years. The Fountain Workshop has clients across the UK, but it's also gaining an international presence with clients in Central Africa and Mustique. In fact, it recently secured a £2 million contract in Copenhagen, its largest single contract outside the UK to date.

The success of the business hasn't gone unnoticed. The Fountain Workshop won the 1998 Medway Small Business of the Year Award and was runner up in 1997. It also won the Pride of Medway Award in 2000 and has received various civic-trust awards for its contribution to the quality and appearance of the environment.

Fountain Workshop Ltd
Ian Kirkpatrick and David Bracey
T: +44 (0)1634 829 820
E: sales@fountains.co.uk
W: www.fountains.co.uk

'We made the leather that was used for costumes in the Harry Potter films.'

Describe yourself in three words.
Tanner, businessman, family man.

Best thing about Medway?
Medway's location is excellent. It has convenient access to both London and the Continent. We make frequent use of Ebbsfleet International Station.

What has been your most unusual commission?
We made the leather that was used for costumes in the Harry Potter films.

Your earliest memory?
The evocative smell of leather.

Who do you admire most?
Dr Habibi and his colleagues who were working at the Great Ormond Street Children's Hospital when my daughter was a baby and needed them most.

The best piece of advice you've been given?
'Be adaptable'. Particularly in the leather industry, where new fashion and design trends are constantly emerging. You have to respond and be innovative.

Your most overused phrase?
It's all part of life's rich pageant!

What do you consider to be your greatest achievement?
My two children, Kate and Luke.

Paul Hanson always knew he wanted to be a tanner. It was his father's trade, and from an early age he was fascinated by the beautiful products that could be created using leather. He gained his early experience as an apprentice to a leather craftsman in Walsall before becoming Managing Director of Hanson-Tower in the 1990s. Hanson-Tower is a family business; Paul and his team of twenty pride themselves on creating beautiful, high-quality English leather that is used in a diverse range of products from car interiors and upmarket leather goods to pet collars, saddles and bridles. More recently they have diversified into architectural leatherwork such as floors and walls.

The company was originally founded in 1973 in London's old leather-production area of Bermondsey on the south bank of the Thames overlooking the Tower of London. In 1982 it relocated to Strood where it now resides, nestled on the banks of the River Medway overlooking Rochester Castle!

Hanson–Tower has a diverse client base, trading extensively in the UK and Europe, with customers in China and Japan purchasing large volumes of its renowned traditional English bridle leather. But while its products and techniques are steeped in tradition, Paul firmly believes in moving with the times. The company has a flexible approach to product delivery and often works to tight deadlines, turning goods around in seventy-two hours from receipt of order to dispatch of goods. It also works extensively with interior and fashion clients, delivering on designers' specifications and collaborating on projects that are often highly innovative.

Green issues are also on the company's agenda, and Hanson-Tower has introduced production methods that have minimum impact on the environment. For the same reason, all its leather is vegetable tanned using natural products, ideally mimosa.

With its assessment to BS EN ISO 9001:2000 firmly under its belt, Hanson-Tower is dedicated to delivering impeccable work standards that will stand it in good stead for the future. As the architectural side of its business continues to grow, Paul predicts that increasing amounts future business will come from fitting out more interiors for luxury hotels, bars, shops and even yachts – high-grade clients for a high-grade company.

Hanson-Tower
Paul Hanson
T: +44 (0)1634 713363
E: Kelly@hanson-tower.com
W: www.hanson-tower.co.uk

Rope has been manufactured at Chatham's Historic Dockyard since 1618.

BSL Gas Technologies

'There has to be an affordable and sustainable alternative to oil. Most people have no idea of the extent we really depend on it.'

Describe yourself in three words.
Kind, tolerant, messy.

What inspires you?
Finding the simple solution to a difficult problem.

What puts a smile on your face?
Opening the throttle on my motorcycle!

Best thing about Medway?
It has a good motorway network (albeit too crowded) and excellent access to the Continent by road and rail.

Who do you admire most?
As an engineer I should say Brunel, but at the moment it's Valentino Rossi. He's a true world champion who can still have fun and break the rules.

Your most overused phrase?
When driving in bad weather: it's brighter ahead!

What in your opinion will be the 'next big thing'?
There has to be an affordable and sustainable alternative to oil. Most people have no idea of the extent we really depend on this fuel; it goes way beyond transport and heating and plays a part in almost everything we do or use.

Your philosophy in a nutshell?
To coin a phrase from the *Reader's Digest*: 'Laughter is the best medicine ...'

BSL Gas Technologies' website states that the company mixes knowledge and resources to deliver thought-provoking industrial gas solutions, and it's clear that BSL is technologically advanced. As the manufacturer of a huge range of gas-mixing equipment covering beer and soft-drink dispensing, food packing and robot-welding markets, it is a leader in its field. In fact, most pubs, clubs and restaurants across the UK have a BSL mixer in their cellar. Mixed gas is also widely used in food-packing applications – another specialist area for this company.

Graham Whibley is one of the founder members who established BSL Gas Technologies eighteen years ago. He has an impressive forty years' experience of manufacturing in Medway. Engineering is in his blood – at a mere eight years old he was helping his father repair the family car! After a stint studying at Medway College of Technology, he gained an HND and CEI Part Two in Mechanical Engineering and became a chartered engineer before setting up BSL.

In keeping with the current trend for green and sustainable initiatives, BSL has been busy implementing schemes designed to reduce carbon-dioxide leaks in their pipework systems. This equipment is linked via a GPS system to BSL's offices in Rochester where weekly reports and schedules are produced, assisting the maintenance teams with finding and repairing system leaks. This system has been proven to reduce carbon-dioxide emissions considerably. The company takes its production values seriously and was the winner of the 2007 Medway Business Awards for its 'Contribution to Medway'. Although material costs have shot up considerably, BSL has remained in business by giving its customers the products and services they need.

The company has an extensive client base, which includes all of the major blue-chip industrial gas supply companies such as BOC. Starting with only one customer in the UK, BSL has expanded rapidly and now sells all over Europe as well as to Australia, China, India, South Africa and New Zealand.

BSL Gas Technologies Ltd
Graham Whibley
T: +44 (0)1634 661 100
E: Graham@bslgastech.com
W: www.bslgastech.com

Tatty Devine

'Quality is important to us – having production here in Medway means we have full control.'

Who or what inspires you?
Everything! We are inspired mostly by each other, our friends, our childhood and time spent together at art school.

Has the manufacturing industry changed since you've been in business?
We have always kept our manufacturing in-house. Quality is important to us – having production here in Medway means we have full control. We also know that our processes and conditions are ethical. Having said that, it is getting harder to source materials made in the UK.

What can't you live without?
Chamomile tea (Harriet), coffee (Rosie) and Radio 4 in the morning.

What's the best piece of advice you've ever received?
Stick to what you believe in.

What do you consider to be your greatest achievement?
Getting Tatty Devine to the level it is at. Selling internationally, opening two shops and employing twenty people.

Your philosophy in a nutshell?
All that really matters is our health and happiness.

Rosie Wolfenden and Harriet Vine met while studying Fine Art at Chelsea. They had originally planned to become artists, but, as luck would have it, Harriet found some bags of fabric samples on the way home from the pub. She then made some leather cuffs, sold them at London's Portobello and Spitalfields markets, and in 1999 Tatty Devine was born!

These two fine artists turned jewellers need no introduction in the fashion world – *Vogue*, *Marie Claire* and the *Observer* regularly feature their products. Their jewellery is fun and quirky, referencing retro themes and pop nostalgia. Dinosaur necklaces, Rubik's Cube bracelets and water-pistol brooches are typical of their trademark eclectic designs. A personalised-name necklace service is also offered. They specialise in sheet acrylic with the additional use of wood, beads and leather. In terms of sustainability, they recycle all their acrylic off-cuts, which gets made into black acrylic. In fact, Tatty Devine started the trend for laser-cut acrylic jewellery, which has since been imitated by many.

In a short space of time they have expanded rapidly: 2001 saw the girls launch their first official collection at London Fashion Week; in 2003 they began showing at Paris Fashion Week; while in 2006 they made their debut at New York Fashion Week. Tatty Devine's jewellery and accessories can be found in over 100 stockists worldwide, and they now employ twenty people. The girls oversee all aspects of the business from design to production to retail. They have a gallery and press showroom, two London boutiques (in Soho and Brick Lane) and a new office and workshop in Gillingham.

Harriet is from Rochester originally, so relocating the studio to Medway was a natural choice. Established in February 2008, the Medway production unit was set up with a view to expanding their team and facilities. Two collections are launched every year, and their 'Best Of' collection gathers together all the popular pieces. Clients include the V&A, the Tate Gallery, Harvey Nichols and Browns Focus.

Tatty Devine
Rosie Wolfenden, Lynda Phillips
T: +44 (0)1634 578 508
E: rosie@tattydevine.com
lynda@tattydevine.com
W: www.tattydevine.com

Jubilee Clips

'There is an amazing skill base here, and people are very resourceful. Perhaps this ethic comes from the dockyard and the Royal Engineers' barracks.'

What inspires you?
Watching a huge container crammed with tens or hundreds of thousands of Jubilee Clips leaving the premises and knowing that they are destined for the other side of the world.

Has the manufacturing industry changed since you've been in business?
Safety concerns barely existed in the early days of the company. Whereas modern business practices realise the importance of protecting all resources, including people.

Best thing about Medway?
The people. There is an amazing skill base here, and people are very resourceful. Perhaps this ethic comes from the dockyard and the Royal Engineers' barracks.

What's the best piece of advice you've ever received?
If you can't make a mistake, you can't make anything. Learn from your mistakes ...

Your most overused phrases?
We have a few slogans: 'quality matters more' and 'beware of imitations' sum us up quite well. Our clips are high quality, and others do try to copy them.

Your greatest achievement?
We have recently consolidated staff and equipment from six sites into one. It was a huge effort but took just ten months with little or no impact on our supply to customers; a great credit to the efforts of all involved.

In 1921 ex-Royal Navy officer Commander Lumley Robinson invented the worm-drive hose clip. He didn't know it at the time, but his Jubilee Clip was to become an iconic, world-class product. Fortunately, he patented his invention and founded L. Robinson & Co. (Gillingham) Ltd. The company has been manufacturing Jubilee® Clips in Gillingham ever since. Despite enjoying worldwide success, the company remains a family business; the board consists of descendants and relatives of Commander Lumley. The company's logo design has remained untouched since 1921 and, what's more, it even manufactures its own specialist machinery on-site!

If a hose clip is faulty it can have disastrous results. In recent years the market has been swamped by a plethora of cheap, mass-produced clips. Complex, high-tech machinery can become immobilised when a small component such as a hose clip malfunctions, causing considerable damage and safety issues. The chances are that the clip will be sitting in an awkward place, which can increase the time needed to fix the problem. However, this issue doesn't arise with Jubilee® Clips, as it uses premium-grade materials and employs a stringent quality-control process. All product ranges are systematically checked from raw material to finished product and conform to the latest EU directives.

Jubilee® was instrumental in the formulation of the original British Standard back in 1963. Because the business is a tight-knit family concern, the directors ensure that quality is never compromised, which, in turn, sets them apart from their competitors. In addition to the British Standard Kitemark, the company is Lloyd's Type approved, has ISO and Ministry of Defence approval and meets the British standard for aerospace hose clips. Furthermore, it aims to work in a socially, ethically and environmentally responsible way, ensuring that manufacturing processes conform to environmental legislation. In terms of sustainability, the company recycles scrap metal, paper and card and has also upped its green credentials by changing methods of treating the metal used and improving the corrosion resistance of the product.

Jubilee® Clips are used on practically every continent. The UK is a key market, but they also thrive in areas such as the UAE and Japan – which are notorious for their exacting standards. The extension of the EU has also seen demand for products in newer member states, including Estonia and Poland, while 2007 saw Jubilee® Clips export directly to China. They also have a branch in Germany, Jubilee Clips Deutschland GmbH, which was established in 1982.

Jubilee Clips
Suzanne Barnard
T: +44 (0)1634 281 200
E: sales@jubileeclips.co.uk
W: www.jubileeclips.co.uk

Made In Medway 2
info@madeinmedway.com
www.madeinmedway.com
Made In...
www.madeinltd.com

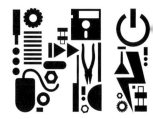

By Steve Rowland
& Bianca Donnelly